A BEGINNER'S GUIDE TO LASER ENGRAVING

Laser Engraving 101

1

Table of Contents

Chapter 1: Introduction to Laser Engraving

Whether you're a hobbyist looking to personalize gifts or an aspiring entrepreneur considering a laser engraving business, "A Beginner's Guide to Laser Engraving" is your comprehensive companion to mastering this exciting and versatile technology. From understanding the fundamentals to creating intricate designs and even exploring the world of entrepreneurship, this book will equip you with the knowledge and skills you need to embark on your laser engraving journey with confidence.

What is Laser Engraving?

Laser engraving is a technology that uses a high-powered laser beam to etch or engrave a surface. It is a precise and versatile method for creating intricate designs, patterns, text, or images on a wide variety of materials, including wood, metal, glass, acrylic, plastic, leather, and more. Laser engraving is commonly used in industrial, commercial, and hobbyist applications for various purposes, such as personalization, branding, signage, and decorative art.

Here's how laser engraving typically works:

1. Laser Source: A laser engraving machine consists of a high-energy laser source, such as a CO_2, fiber, or diode laser. The type of laser used depends on the material being engraved and the desired result.

2. Focusing Optics: The laser beam is directed through a series of focusing optics, including lenses and mirrors, to concentrate it into a highly focused point.

3. Material Placement: The material to be engraved is placed within the laser engraving machine. The machine may have a movable worktable that can move the material beneath the focused laser beam or a galvanometer system that rapidly directs the laser beam across the material's surface.

4. Laser Etching: The focused laser beam is precisely controlled by computer software. It moves across the material's surface, vaporizing or ablating a tiny amount of material with each pass. The path of the laser beam follows the design or pattern programmed into the software.

5. Depth and Detail: The depth and level of detail in the engraving are determined by the power and speed of the laser, as well as the material's characteristics. Deeper engravings require more laser power and slower speeds, while finer details may necessitate higher precision and slower speeds.

6. Cooling and Exhaust: Laser engraving machines often use cooling systems to dissipate the heat generated during the engraving process. Additionally, an exhaust system helps remove any fumes or debris produced during the engraving.

7. Finished Product: Once the laser engraving is complete, the material is removed from the machine. The engraved area will have a permanent mark or design, depending on the depth and material used.

Laser engraving offers several advantages, including high precision, repeatability, and the ability to work with a wide range of materials. It's commonly used for personalizing items like trophies, jewelry, and electronics, creating intricate artwork, producing labels and barcodes, and adding branding or serial numbers to industrial components. The versatility and speed of laser engraving make it a popular choice in various industries and applications.

Brief History of Laser Engraving

Laser engraving is a relatively modern technology, and its history is intertwined with the development and evolution of lasers. Here's a brief overview of the key milestones in the history of laser engraving:

1. Invention of the Laser (1950s):

    - The development of the laser (Light Amplification by Stimulated Emission of Radiation) began in the mid-20th century. In 1958, Arthur Schawlow and Charles Townes published a paper outlining the theoretical principles of the laser.

2. First Working Laser (1960):

    - In 1960, Theodore Maiman constructed the first functional laser using a synthetic ruby crystal. This marked the birth of practical laser technology.

3. Early Laser Applications (1960s and 1970s):

    - In the early years of lasers, they were primarily used for scientific research and military applications. The concept of using lasers for material processing and engraving had not yet been widely explored.

4. Laser Engraving Development (1980s):

    - The 1980s saw the emergence of laser engraving as a practical industrial technology. Early laser engraving systems were developed and used in various industries, particularly for marking and engraving on metals.

5. Advancements in Laser Technology (1990s):

    - During the 1990s, advancements in laser technology, including the development of more efficient and versatile lasers like CO_2 and Nd:YAG lasers, made laser engraving more accessible and cost-effective.

6. Desktop Laser Engraving (2000s):

    - The 21st century brought about the development of smaller, more affordable laser engraving machines suitable for desktop and small business use. These machines expanded the accessibility of laser engraving for a wider range of applications, including engraving on wood, acrylic, and plastics.

7. Advancements in Software and Control (2000s and beyond):

    - Alongside hardware improvements, there were significant advancements in laser engraving software and control systems, making it easier to create and manipulate designs for engraving.

8. Diverse Material Compatibility (Present):

- Today, laser engraving technology has matured, and it can work with a wide range of materials, from metals and glass to wood, leather, and even certain plastics. Different types of lasers, such as CO_2, fiber, and diode lasers, are used depending on the material and application.

9. Personalization and Industrial Use (Present):

   - Laser engraving has become a popular method for personalizing products, adding branding, creating custom designs, and marking parts in various industries, including manufacturing, jewelry, signage, and art.

Overall, laser engraving has evolved from a scientific curiosity in the 1960s to a versatile and widely adopted technology with a wide range of industrial and consumer applications today. Its continued development and innovations in laser sources and control systems are likely to expand its capabilities even further in the future.

Applications of Laser Engraving

Laser engraving is a versatile technology with a wide range of applications across various industries. Its precision, speed, and ability to work with various materials make it a valuable tool for many purposes. Here are some common applications for laser engraving:

1. **Personalization and Customization:**

   - Laser engraving is often used to personalize and customize products. This includes engraving names, initials, dates, or personal messages on items like jewelry, gifts, awards, and promotional items.

2. **Jewelry Design and Marking:**

   - Jewelers use laser engraving to create intricate designs on metal surfaces, such as rings, bracelets, and pendants. It's also used for marking precious metals with purity information and logos.

3. **Industrial Marking and Branding:**

   - Manufacturers use laser engraving to mark serial numbers, barcodes, and logos on industrial components, tools, and machinery. This helps with tracking and branding of products.

4. **Signage and Labels:**

   - Laser engraving is employed to create high-quality signage and labels on materials like acrylic, wood, and metal. It's commonly used in architectural signage, nameplates, and product labeling.

5. **Woodworking and Cabinetry:**

   - Woodworkers use laser engraving for adding decorative details, custom patterns, and text on wooden furniture, cabinetry, and decorative items. It's also used for engraving woodcut artwork.

6. **Awards and Trophies:**
   - Laser engraving is popular in the awards and trophy industry for creating plaques, trophies, and medals. It allows for detailed and precise customization.

7. **Glass Engraving:**
   - Glassware and glass products can be engraved with intricate designs, logos, and text for both decorative and branding purposes.

8. **Acrylic and Plastic Marking:**
   - Laser engraving on acrylic and plastic materials is common for creating intricate designs, product prototypes, and signage.

9. **Leather Embossing and Marking:**
   - Leather goods manufacturers use laser engraving for embossing logos, patterns, and designs on products such as wallets, belts, and bags.

10. **Art and Crafts:**
    - Artists and craft enthusiasts use laser engraving to create intricate artwork on various materials, including paper, wood, and acrylic.

11. **Medical and Dental Applications:**
    - Laser engraving is used in the medical and dental fields for marking surgical instruments, dental implants, and prosthetics.

12. **Electronics and PCBs:**
    - Laser engraving is used for marking and cutting printed circuit boards (PCBs) and electronic components.

13. **Memorial Plaques and Monuments:**
    - Laser engraving is employed to create memorial plaques, headstones, and monuments with personalized text, photos, and designs.

14. **Architectural Models:**
    - Architects and model makers use laser engraving to create detailed architectural models and prototypes.

15. **Food and Beverage Industry:**
    - In the food and beverage industry, laser engraving is used for labeling and branding items like wine bottles, cutting boards, and personalized cake toppers.

These are just some of the many applications of laser engraving. The technology's versatility and precision make it valuable across a broad spectrum of industries and creative endeavors. It continues to find new applications as technology evolves and materials science advances.

Why Choose Laser Engraving?

Choosing laser engraving as a business can be a lucrative and rewarding venture for several reasons:

1. **Versatility:** Laser engraving can work with a wide range of materials, including wood, metal, glass, acrylic, leather, plastics, and more. This versatility allows you to serve diverse markets and cater to various customer needs.

2. **Precision and Detail:** Laser engraving offers exceptional precision and detail, enabling you to create intricate designs, fine text, and complex patterns with high accuracy. This quality is often valued by customers looking for personalized or custom items.

3. **Customization:** Personalization is a significant trend in various industries, from gifts and jewelry to promotional products and industrial components. Laser engraving allows you to offer customized solutions, which can command higher prices and build customer loyalty.

4. **Speed and Efficiency:** Laser engraving is a fast and efficient process, allowing you to complete projects quickly and fulfill customer orders promptly. This efficiency can help you take on a high volume of work and meet tight deadlines.

5. **Low Operating Costs:** Laser engraving machines have relatively low operating costs compared to some other manufacturing and customization methods. Once you have the equipment in place, the primary expenses are maintenance, electricity, and materials.

6. **Scalability:** As your business grows, you can scale up by investing in more laser engraving machines or expanding your product offerings. The technology is conducive to both small-scale and large-scale production.

7. **Diverse Market Opportunities:** Laser engraving serves numerous markets, including retail, industrial, promotional, artistic, and more. This diversity allows you to target different niches and adapt to changing market trends.

8. **Eco-Friendly:** Laser engraving is an environmentally friendly process. It produces minimal waste, doesn't involve the use of harmful chemicals, and is energy-efficient compared to other manufacturing processes.

9. **Profit Margins:** Laser engraving businesses can often command healthy profit margins, especially for custom or high-end products. Customers are willing to pay more for personalized and finely crafted items.

10. **Creative Outlet:** If you have a passion for design and creativity, laser engraving can be a satisfying and fulfilling business. You get to work on a wide variety of projects and see your artistic ideas come to life.

11. **Low Entry Barriers:** While the initial investment in laser engraving equipment can be substantial, the entry barriers are relatively low compared to many other manufacturing businesses. With the right training and business plan, you can get started relatively quickly.

12. **Online Sales Opportunities:** In addition to local customers, you can tap into the global market by selling laser-engraved products online through e-commerce platforms, reaching a broader customer base.

13. **Repeat Business:** Satisfied customers often return for more customized items or recommend your services to others, fostering repeat business and word-of-mouth marketing.

14. **Innovation Potential:** The laser engraving industry continues to evolve with technological advancements. Staying up to date with the latest laser technology and software can open up new possibilities and competitive advantages.

While laser engraving can be a promising business, it's important to conduct thorough market research, invest in quality equipment, and develop a strong marketing and customer service strategy to succeed in this competitive field.

Chapter 2: Getting Started

Choosing the Right Laser Engraving Machine

Choosing the right laser engraving machine is a critical decision for starting or expanding a laser engraving business. The choice depends on various factors, including your budget, intended applications, materials you'll work with, and your long-term business goals. Here are steps to help you select the right laser engraving machine:

1. **Identify Your Needs and Applications:**

   - Determine the primary applications for your laser engraving machine. Are you focused on engraving metal, wood, glass, or a combination of materials? Are you specializing in personalized items, industrial marking, or artistic projects?

2. **Budget Considerations:**

   - Establish a budget for your laser engraving machine. Prices can vary significantly based on the machine's size, power, and capabilities. Be realistic about your budget, but also consider the long-term return on investment.

3. **Machine Size and Workspace:**

   - Assess the available space in your workspace. The size of the machine you choose should fit comfortably within your working area. Additionally, consider the size of the materials you'll be working with.

4. **Laser Type:**

   - Choose the appropriate type of laser for your applications:

     - **CO2 Lasers:** Ideal for engraving non-metallic materials like wood, acrylic, and glass.

     - **Fiber Lasers:** Suited for engraving and marking metals, including stainless steel, aluminum, and brass.

     - **Diode Lasers:** Generally used for smaller-scale and lower-power applications on various materials.

5. **Laser Power and Speed:**

   - Consider the laser power required for your applications. Higher power lasers can cut and engrave thicker materials more quickly but may have a higher initial cost.

6. **Resolution and Precision:**

   - Assess the engraving resolution and precision you need. Machines with higher resolution and precision are better for detailed and intricate work.

7. **Software and Control:**

- Evaluate the included software and control system. User-friendly software can make a significant difference in your workflow. Ensure it supports the file formats you'll be working with.

8. **Support and Training:**

   - Research the manufacturer's reputation for customer support and training. Good customer support can be crucial if you encounter technical issues or have questions about using the machine.

9. **Maintenance and Reliability:**

   - Inquire about the maintenance requirements and reliability of the machine. Frequent breakdowns can disrupt your business operations.

10. **Safety Features:**

    - Laser engraving machines use high-powered lasers, so safety features are essential. Ensure the machine has proper safety interlocks, enclosure options, and meets safety standards and regulations.

11. **Warranty and Service:**

    - Check the warranty terms and conditions. Some manufacturers offer extended warranties and maintenance packages.

12. **User Reviews and References:**

    - Look for user reviews and seek references from other businesses that have purchased the same or similar machines. Hearing about others' experiences can be valuable.

13. **Future Expansion:**

    - Consider your long-term business goals. Choose a machine that can grow with your business, allowing for potential upgrades or additional machines as your business expands.

14. **Local Regulations:**

    - Familiarize yourself with local regulations and permits related to operating a laser engraving machine. Ensure that your chosen machine complies with safety and environmental standards in your area.

15. **Demo and Testing:**

    - Whenever possible, request a demonstration or testing of the machine before making a final decision. This can help you assess its performance and suitability for your needs.

Choosing the right laser engraving machine requires careful consideration of your specific requirements and business objectives. Taking the time to research, evaluate options, and potentially seek expert advice can lead to a successful investment that supports your business growth.

Safety Precautions

Laser engraving involves the use of high-powered lasers, and as such, it's essential to prioritize safety when operating these machines. Failure to follow safety precautions can lead to accidents, injuries, or damage to equipment. Here are important laser engraving safety precautions to keep in mind:

1. **Read and Understand the User Manual:**

   - Before operating a laser engraving machine, thoroughly read and understand the user manual provided by the manufacturer. Familiarize yourself with the machine's specific safety features and recommendations.

2. **Training and Certification:**

   - Ensure that operators are properly trained and certified in the safe operation of laser engraving equipment. Training should cover not only how to use the machine but also safety procedures and emergency protocols.

3. **Personal Protective Equipment (PPE):**

   - Wear appropriate personal protective equipment (PPE), which may include safety glasses, laser safety goggles specific to the laser wavelength used, and protective clothing. Ensure that PPE is in good condition and provides adequate protection.

4. **Laser Safety Interlocks:**

   - Ensure that all safety interlocks and mechanisms are functioning correctly. These interlocks are designed to prevent laser operation when safety enclosures or doors are open.

5. **Control Access:**

   - Restrict access to the laser engraving area to authorized personnel only. Use key locks or access codes to prevent unauthorized use.

6. **Emergency Stop (E-Stop) Button:**

   - Know the location of the emergency stop button, and make sure it is easily accessible. Familiarize all operators with its use, and ensure it functions properly.

7. **Ventilation and Air Quality:**

   - Maintain proper ventilation to remove fumes and particulates generated during the engraving process. Use an appropriate exhaust system to ensure good air quality in the workspace.

8. **Material Compatibility:**

   - Ensure that the materials you are engraving are safe to use with your laser engraving machine. Some materials can release toxic fumes when engraved. Check the material safety data sheet (MSDS) for each material.

9. **Fire Safety:**

- Keep fire safety equipment, such as fire extinguishers, readily available in case of a fire caused by a laser mishap. Avoid engraving flammable materials without appropriate safety measures in place.

10. **Laser Classification:**

- Be aware of the laser classification of your machine, as it determines the potential hazards and safety requirements. Ensure that your machine complies with laser safety standards and regulations.

11. **Signage and Warnings:**

- Post warning signs and labels in the laser engraving area to alert personnel to the presence of a laser and remind them of safety precautions.

12. **Eye Protection:**

- Never look directly into the laser beam or expose your eyes to scattered laser light. Always wear appropriate laser safety goggles designed for the specific wavelength of the laser being used.

13. **Secure Loose Items:**

- Ensure that workpieces and materials are securely clamped or positioned to prevent movement during engraving. Loose items can disrupt the engraving process or create safety hazards.

14. **Maintenance and Inspections:**

- Regularly inspect and maintain the laser engraving machine. Replace worn or damaged components promptly and keep the machine clean and free of debris.

15. **Emergency Procedures:**

- Establish and communicate emergency procedures to all operators. These procedures should include steps to follow in case of fire, machine malfunctions, or injuries.

Safety should always be a top priority when operating a laser engraving machine. Following these precautions and best practices helps ensure the well-being of operators and the safe operation of the equipment. Additionally, compliance with local safety regulations and standards is essential for a safe and productive workspace.

Setting up Your Workspace

Setting up your laser engraving workspace is crucial for ensuring safety, efficiency, and the overall success of your laser engraving business. Here are steps to help you create a well-organized and safe workspace:

1. **Choose an Appropriate Location:**

- Select a dedicated and well-ventilated area for your laser engraving workspace. Ideally, it should be a separate room or an isolated section within a larger workspace to minimize distractions and safety risks.

2. **Ensure Adequate Ventilation:**

   - Install an exhaust system to remove fumes, dust, and smoke generated during the engraving process. The ventilation system should direct contaminants safely outdoors or through proper filtration.

3. **Lighting:**

   - Ensure good lighting in the workspace to allow for clear visibility of the engraving area and controls. Proper lighting is essential for quality control and safety.

4. **Workbench and Surface:**

   - Set up a sturdy workbench or table to place the laser engraving machine. Ensure that it's level and capable of supporting the weight of the machine. A clean and smooth work surface is essential for precise engraving.

5. **Safety Enclosure:**

   - If your laser engraving machine doesn't come with a built-in safety enclosure, consider installing one around the machine. The enclosure should have safety interlocks and provide protection from laser radiation.

6. **Personal Protective Equipment (PPE) Storage:**

   - Designate an area for storing PPE, such as laser safety goggles, safety glasses, and protective clothing. Ensure that PPE is easily accessible to operators.

7. **Organize Materials:**

   - Arrange materials and workpieces in an organized manner. Use shelves, bins, or storage cabinets to keep materials sorted and readily available. Ensure that flammable materials are stored away from potential laser hazards.

8. **Emergency Equipment:**

   - Have emergency equipment on hand, including a fire extinguisher, first aid kit, and an eye wash station, if applicable.

9. **Tool Organization:**

   - Organize engraving tools, maintenance tools, and cleaning supplies in a designated area. Ensure that everything is easily accessible when needed.

10. **Electrical Connections:**

- Ensure proper electrical connections and outlets for your laser engraving machine. Use surge protectors or uninterruptible power supplies (UPS) to protect against power fluctuations.

11. **Fire Safety:**

- Implement fire safety measures, such as fire-resistant materials for the workspace and clear pathways for evacuation. Regularly check smoke detectors and fire alarm systems.

12. **Workspace Layout:**

- Arrange equipment and workstations logically, considering the workflow from design to engraving. Ensure that cords and cables are properly managed to prevent tripping hazards.

13. **Training and Procedures:**

- Develop clear operating procedures and safety protocols for your workspace. Ensure that all operators are trained on safety practices and emergency procedures.

14. **Signage:**

- Post safety signs and labels indicating the presence of a laser and specifying safety precautions. Include emergency contact information and the location of safety equipment.

15. **Regular Maintenance:**

- Establish a maintenance schedule for your laser engraving machine and workspace. Regularly clean the machine, check for loose connections, and replace worn parts.

16. **Documentation:**

- Maintain documentation related to machine maintenance, safety inspections, and operator training. This documentation may be required for regulatory compliance and insurance purposes.

17. **Safety Review:**

- Periodically review and assess the safety of your laser engraving workspace to identify and address any potential hazards or safety improvements.

By following these steps and prioritizing safety and organization, you can create a laser engraving workspace that enhances productivity, minimizes risks, and supports the success of your business. Remember to comply with local safety regulations and standards applicable to laser operations in your area.

Materials You Can Engrave

Laser engraving is a versatile technology that can be used to engrave a wide range of materials. The type of laser used, and its power will determine the materials that can be engraved effectively. Here are some common materials that can be engraved using laser engraving:

1. **Wood:** Laser engraving is popular for engraving on wood, including hardwoods, softwoods, and plywood. It's commonly used for woodworking projects, signs, and decorative items.

2. **Acrylic:** Acrylic is a popular material for laser engraving because it produces high-contrast, precise engravings. It's often used for signage, awards, and decorative applications.

3. **Glass:** Laser engraving can create intricate designs and text on glass surfaces, such as glassware, mirrors, and glass panels.

4. **Metal:** Metal engraving is typically done with fiber lasers, which are capable of marking and engraving on materials like stainless steel, aluminum, brass, and copper. Common applications include industrial part marking and personalization of metal items.

5. **Leather:** Leather engraving is used to create patterns, logos, and custom designs on leather products like belts, wallets, and bags.

6. **Plastics:** Various types of plastics, including ABS, acrylic, and polycarbonate, can be engraved with laser technology. Applications range from signage to personalized plastic items.

7. **Stone:** Natural stones like granite and marble can be engraved for decorative purposes, memorials, and architectural projects.

8. **Ceramics and Porcelain:** Laser engraving can create intricate designs on ceramics and porcelain, often used for custom dishware, tiles, and art pieces.

9. **Paper and Cardboard:** Laser engraving can produce delicate and precise patterns on paper and cardboard for artistic and decorative purposes.

10. **Fabric and Textiles:** Laser engraving can etch designs and patterns on fabric and textiles, often used for clothing, accessories, and upholstery.

11. **Rubber:** Laser engraving is used to create stamps, seals, and custom rubber products.

12. **Foam:** Foam materials, such as foam board and foam rubber, can be engraved for various applications, including signage and packaging.

13. **Anodized Aluminum:** Laser engraving can remove the anodized coating from aluminum surfaces, revealing the underlying metal for detailed designs and text.

14. **Cork:** Cork materials can be engraved for custom coasters, bulletin boards, and other decorative items.

15. **Coated Surfaces:** Some materials, like powder-coated or painted metal, can be engraved by removing the surface coating to reveal the underlying material.

t's important to note that the effectiveness of laser engraving on specific materials can vary based on the laser type, power, and settings. Some materials may require specific techniques or precautions, so t's essential to consult the laser machine's user manual and follow manufacturer guidelines when engraving different materials. Additionally, always consider safety precautions, material compatibility, and ventilation when working with laser engraving machines.

Chapter 3: Understanding Laser Technology

How Lasers Work

Laser engraving machines work by using a high-powered laser beam to etch or engrave a surface. The process involves precise control of the laser's intensity, focus, and movement to create intricate designs, patterns, text, or images on various materials. Here's a step-by-step explanation of how laser engraving machines work:

1. **Laser Source:** Laser engraving machines are equipped with a laser source, which can be one of several types, including CO_2 lasers, fiber lasers, or diode lasers. The choice of laser type depends on the material being engraved and the desired results.

2. **Beam Generation:** The laser source generates a high-energy laser beam, which is a concentrated and coherent stream of photons. The laser beam's wavelength and intensity vary depending on the type of laser used.

3. **Focusing Optics:** The laser beam passes through a series of focusing optics, including lenses and mirrors, to concentrate it into a highly focused point. The focusing optics help control the beam's size and ensure that it remains tightly focused on the material's surface.

4. **Material Placement:** The material to be engraved is placed within the laser engraving machine. Some machines have a movable worktable that can move the material beneath the focused laser beam, while others use a galvanometer system that rapidly directs the laser beam across the material's surface.

5. **Laser Etching:** The focused laser beam is precisely controlled by computer software. The software guides the laser beam as it moves across the material's surface, vaporizing or ablating a tiny amount of material with each pass. The path of the laser beam follows the design or pattern programmed into the software.

6. **Depth and Detail Control:** The depth and level of detail in the engraving are determined by several factors:

   - Laser Power: More laser power results in deeper engravings.

   - Laser Speed: Slower engraving speeds can achieve greater depth and finer detail.

   - Material Properties: Different materials respond differently to laser engraving, affecting depth and detail.

7. **Cooling and Exhaust:** Laser engraving machines often have cooling systems to dissipate the heat generated during the engraving process. Additionally, an exhaust system helps remove any fumes or debris produced during the engraving.

8. **Finished Product:** Once the laser engraving is complete, the material is removed from the machine. The engraved area will have a permanent mark or design, depending on the depth and material used.

Laser engraving offers several advantages, including high precision, repeatability, and the ability to work with a wide range of materials. It is commonly used in various industries for purposes such as personalization, branding, signage, and decorative art. The versatility and speed of laser engraving make it a popular choice for a wide range of applications.

Types of Laser Engraving Machines

There are several types of laser engraving machines available, each with its own set of characteristics and applications. The choice of the right type of laser engraving machine depends on factors such as the materials you intend to engrave, the level of precision required, and your budget. Here are the primary types of laser engraving machines:

1. **CO2 Laser Engraving Machines:**

   - CO2 lasers are the most common type of laser used in engraving. They use a carbon dioxide gas mixture as the laser medium.

   - Materials Engraved: CO2 lasers are versatile and can engrave a wide range of non-metallic materials, including wood, acrylic, leather, glass, ceramics, plastics, and more.

   - Applications: Popular for engraving signage, personalized gifts, awards, and decorative items.

2. **Fiber Laser Engraving Machines:**

   - Fiber lasers use a fiber-optic laser source to generate a laser beam. They are highly efficient and suitable for marking and engraving on metals and some plastics.

   - Materials Engraved: Fiber lasers are primarily used for engraving and marking on metals, including stainless steel, aluminum, brass, and copper. They can also mark certain plastics.

   - Applications: Commonly used in industrial applications for part marking, barcoding, and engraving metal components.

3. **Diode Laser Engraving Machines:**

   - Diode lasers use semiconductor diodes as the laser source. They are compact and energy-efficient, making them suitable for smaller-scale applications.

   - Materials Engraved: Diode lasers are used for engraving and marking on various materials, including wood, acrylic, leather, some plastics, and thin metals.

   - Applications: Popular for engraving small-scale personalized items, promotional products, and hobbyist projects.

4. **UV Laser Engraving Machines:**

   - UV (Ultraviolet) lasers use shorter wavelengths compared to CO2 and fiber lasers, which makes them suitable for engraving certain materials with high precision.

- Materials Engraved: UV lasers can engrave on a variety of materials, including glass, certain plastics, ceramics, and some metals.
- Applications: Often used for fine detail engraving on electronic components, glassware, and promotional items.

5. **Green Laser Engraving Machines:**

- Green lasers fall between UV and CO2 lasers in terms of wavelength. They are suitable for some applications where high precision and fine detail are required.
- Materials Engraved: Green lasers can engrave on a range of materials, including plastics, ceramics, certain metals, and some organic materials.
- Applications: Used for applications that demand high precision and fine detail, such as jewelry and small electronic parts.

6. **3D Laser Engraving Machines:**

- These machines are equipped with galvanometer systems that allow them to engrave curved and irregular surfaces, creating three-dimensional effects.
- Materials Engraved: 3D laser engraving machines can work with various materials, including metals, glass, crystal, and acrylic.
- Applications: Commonly used for creating intricate 3D designs and patterns on jewelry, promotional items, and decorative pieces.

Each type of laser engraving machine has its advantages and limitations, so it's essential to select the one that best suits your specific needs and the materials you plan to work with. Additionally, consider factors such as laser power, engraving speed, and software compatibility when choosing a laser engraving machine.

CO2 vs. Fiber Lasers

CO2 and fiber lasers are two common types of lasers used in engraving and marking applications, and each has its own advantages and limitations. The choice between CO2 and fiber lasers depends on the materials you need to engrave and the specific requirements of your application. Here's a comparison of CO2 and fiber lasers:

CO2 Lasers:

1. **Wavelength:** CO2 lasers have a longer wavelength (typically around 10.6 micrometers) compared to fiber lasers. This longer wavelength is well-suited for engraving on non-metallic materials like wood, acrylic, glass, plastics, leather, and ceramics.

2. **Materials:** CO2 lasers are versatile and can engrave a wide range of non-metallic materials, including those that are sensitive to heat.

3. **Engraving Depth:** They are capable of producing deeper engravings on certain materials due to their longer wavelength.

4. **Precision:** CO2 lasers can provide excellent precision and detail, making them suitable for intricate designs and fine text.

5. **Speed:** Engraving with CO2 lasers is generally slower when compared to fiber lasers, especially when engraving on metals.

6. **Efficiency:** CO2 lasers are less energy-efficient than fiber lasers and may have higher operating costs.

7. **Applications:** Common applications for CO2 lasers include engraving and cutting of wood, acrylic, glass, signage, rubber stamps, and artistic projects.

Fiber Lasers:

1. **Wavelength:** Fiber lasers have a shorter wavelength (typically around 1.06 micrometers) that is well-suited for engraving and marking on metals and some plastics.

2. **Materials:** Fiber lasers are primarily used for engraving and marking metals, including stainless steel, aluminum, brass, copper, and some plastics.

3. **Engraving Depth:** They create shallow engravings on metal surfaces, making them ideal for producing high-contrast marks without significantly affecting the material's integrity.

4. **Precision:** Fiber lasers provide excellent precision, making them suitable for intricate designs and fine detail, particularly on metal surfaces.

5. **Speed:** Fiber lasers are faster than CO2 lasers when engraving on metals, which makes them a preferred choice for industrial applications.

6. **Efficiency:** Fiber lasers are energy-efficient and have lower operating costs compared to CO2 lasers.

7. **Applications:** Fiber lasers are commonly used in industrial applications for part marking, barcoding, engraving serial numbers, and branding metal components.

In summary, the choice between CO2 and fiber lasers largely depends on the materials you plan to work with and the nature of your engraving application. CO2 lasers are versatile and suitable for non-metallic materials, while fiber lasers excel in engraving and marking on metals and some plastics. It's important to assess your specific needs and the materials you intend to engrave to determine which type of laser will best meet your requirements.

Power and Wattage Considerations

Laser engraving power, often measured in watts (W), is a crucial factor to consider when choosing a laser engraving machine. The power of the laser affects various aspects of the engraving process, including the speed, depth, and materials that can be engraved. Here are some considerations related to laser engraving power and wattage:

1. **Material Compatibility:**

   - Different materials have varying engraving power requirements. For example, engraving on wood or acrylic may require lower power levels, while engraving on metals typically demands higher power levels. Ensure that the laser power is suitable for the materials you plan to work with.

2. **Engraving Speed:**

- Higher laser power allows for faster engraving speeds. If you need to complete engraving tasks quickly, a higher wattage laser may be preferable.

3. **Depth of Engraving:**

- Laser power influences the depth of the engraving. Higher power lasers can create deeper engravings. This is particularly important for applications where depth is critical, such as creating tactile graphics or embossing.

4. **Detail and Precision:**

- While higher power lasers can produce deeper engravings, they may not be as precise for fine details. Lower power lasers can achieve finer detail work but may take longer to engrave.

5. **Material Safety:**

- Some materials, like plastics, can be sensitive to excessive heat. Using a laser with too much power on such materials may cause melting or damage. It's important to find the right balance between power and material compatibility to avoid undesirable outcomes.

6. **Energy Efficiency:**

- Higher power lasers tend to be less energy-efficient, which can result in higher operating costs. Consider the long-term cost implications of your power choice.

7. **Budget:**

- Laser engraving machines with higher wattage lasers typically come with a higher price tag. Be mindful of your budget constraints when selecting a laser power level.

8. **Versatility:**

- If your engraving needs vary across a wide range of materials and applications, you may want to consider a laser engraving machine with adjustable power settings or interchangeable laser sources. This allows you to adapt to different tasks without needing multiple machines.

9. **Regulations and Safety:**

- Depending on your location and the power of your laser, you may need to comply with specific safety regulations and standards. Higher power lasers may require additional safety measures.

10. **Training and Expertise:**

- Operating high-power lasers may require more extensive training and experience in laser safety and operation. Ensure that you and your team are adequately trained for the laser power you choose.

When selecting the right laser engraving power and wattage for your application, it's essential to strike a balance between speed, precision, material compatibility, and cost considerations. Consider conducting tests and experiments on sample materials to determine the optimal laser power settings for your specific engraving needs.

Formulas for Calculating Laser Engraving Speeds

Calculating laser engraving speeds involves several factors, including the material being engraved, the laser power, the type of laser, and the desired depth or quality of the engraving. While there is no one-size-fits-all formula due to the variability of these factors, you can use the following general guidelines and considerations to estimate laser engraving speeds:

1. **Material Characteristics:**
   - Different materials have varying engraving characteristics, including hardness, density, and thermal conductivity. Softer materials like wood and acrylic generally engrave faster than harder materials like metals.

2. **Laser Power:**
   - The power of the laser (measured in watts) directly impacts engraving speed. Higher laser power can engrave faster, but it may also affect the depth and quality of the engraving. The relationship between laser power and speed is not linear; doubling the power doesn't necessarily double the speed.

3. **Laser Type:**
   - The type of laser (CO2, fiber, diode, etc.) affects engraving speed. Fiber lasers, for example, are faster than CO2 lasers when engraving metals.

4. **Engraving Depth and Quality:**
   - The desired depth and quality of the engraving play a role in determining the engraving speed. Deeper engravings typically require slower speeds, as the laser needs more time to remove material.

5. **Material Masking:**
   - Some materials may require masking with tape or other protective coatings before engraving. This masking can affect the engraving speed as the laser must first remove the masking material.

6. **Resolution and Detail:**
   - Engraving speed may need to be adjusted based on the level of detail and resolution required for the design. Finer details often require slower speeds to maintain precision.

7. **Scanner or Galvanometer Speed:**

- The speed of the laser scanner or galvanometer system can also influence engraving speed. Faster scanners can move the laser beam more quickly across the material.

8. **Trial and Error:**

   - Often, determining the ideal engraving speed for a specific material and design involves a process of trial and error. You may need to perform test engravings at various speeds to find the optimal balance between speed and quality.

There isn't a single formula to calculate engraving speed because it depends on multiple variables. However, most laser engraving machines come with software that allows you to adjust speed settings based on these factors. The best approach is to consult the user manual of your specific laser engraving machine and experiment with different settings to find the speed that achieves your desired results while maintaining the quality of the engraving.

Formulas For Converting Speed

Inches per Minute to Inches per Second

Converting speeds from inches per minute (in/min) to inches per second (in/sec) is a straightforward process. To convert, you can use the following formula:

$$Speed\ (in/sec) = \frac{Speed\ (in/min)}{60}$$

Here's how the conversion works:

1. Take the speed in inches per minute (in/min).

2. Divide it by 60 to convert it to inches per second (in/sec).

For example, if you have a speed of 120 inches per minute (in/min), you can convert it to inches per second (in/sec) as follows:

$$Speed\ (in/sec) = \frac{120\ in/min}{60} = 2\ in/sec$$

So, a speed of 120 inches per minute is equivalent to 2 inches per second.

Inches Per Minute to Millimeters per Second

To convert speeds from inches per minute (in/min) to millimeters per second (mm/s), you can use the following conversion factor:

1 inch = 25.4 millimeters 1 minute = 60 seconds

So, the conversion formula is:

$$Speed\ (mm/s) = \frac{Speed\ (in/min) \times 25.4}{60}$$

Here's how to perform the conversion:

1. Take the speed in inches per minute (in/min).

2. Multiply it by 25.4 to convert inches to millimeters.

3. Divide the result by 60 to convert minutes to seconds.

For example, if you have a speed of 120 inches per minute (in/min), you can convert it to millimeters per second (mm/s) as follows:

Speed (mm/s)=120 in/min×25.460≈50.8 mm/sSpeed (mm/s)=60120in/min×25.4≈50.8mm/s

So, a speed of 120 inches per minute is approximately equivalent to 50.8 millimeters per second.

Chapter 4: Designing for Laser Engraving

Choosing or Creating Designs

Choosing or creating designs for laser engraving is an important aspect of the process, as it directly impacts the outcome of your engraving projects. Whether you're engraving for personal or business purposes, here are some tips for selecting or creating designs for laser engraving:

1. **Understand the Material:** Consider the material you'll be engraving on. Different materials have varying characteristics and engraving capabilities. Some materials are better suited for fine details, while others work well with bold designs. Understanding the material's limitations and potential will guide your design choices.

2. **Design Software:** Familiarize yourself with design software that is compatible with your laser engraving machine. Popular options include Adobe Illustrator, CorelDRAW, AutoCAD, and various CAD software for 3D engraving.

3. **Vector Graphics:** Vector graphics are ideal for laser engraving because they can be scaled without losing quality. Design your artwork in vector format to ensure sharp and precise engravings.

4. **Design Principles:** Apply design principles such as balance, contrast, and simplicity to your designs. Clear and well-structured designs often result in more visually appealing engravings.

5. **Image Resolution:** If working with raster images (like photographs), ensure that the image resolution is high enough to produce a detailed engraving. A resolution of 300 dots per inch (DPI) is typically suitable.

6. **Customization:** Personalized items are popular in laser engraving. Consider offering customizable designs that allow customers to add names, dates, or messages to the engraving.

7. **Testing:** Before engraving on a final product, run test engravings on scrap materials to evaluate how your design will appear on the chosen material. This helps identify any adjustments needed for optimal results.

8. **Safety:** Be mindful of safety concerns, especially when engraving on materials that produce toxic fumes or dust. Design your projects in a way that minimizes health and safety risks.

9. **Font Selection:** Choose fonts carefully, especially for text-based engravings. Fonts should be legible and appropriate for the occasion or purpose of the engraving. Experiment with different fonts to find the most suitable one.

10. **Logo and Branding:** If you're using laser engraving for business, create a distinctive logo or branding elements that can be consistently applied to your products. A well-designed logo can enhance brand recognition.

11. **Artistic Creativity:** For artistic or decorative projects, let your creativity shine. Experiment with various design elements, patterns, and styles to create unique and eye-catching engravings.

12. **Size Considerations:** Keep in mind the size of your engraving area and the proportions of your design. Ensure that your design fits within the available space and maintains its intended aspect ratio.

13. **File Formats:** Save your designs in the appropriate file formats that your laser engraving software or machine accepts. Common formats include SVG, AI, DXF, and BMP.

14. **Copyright and Licensing:** If you're using pre-designed graphics, images, or fonts, make sure you have the necessary permissions or licenses to use them for commercial purposes.

15. **Feedback and Collaboration:** If you're working on custom projects, collaborate closely with your clients to understand their vision and preferences. Solicit feedback to ensure the final design aligns with their expectations.

Remember that practice and experience play a significant role in becoming proficient at choosing or creating designs for laser engraving. As you gain more experience, you'll develop a better understanding of what works best for different materials and applications.

Preparing Vector Graphics

Preparing vector graphics for laser engraving involves several important steps to ensure that your designs are suitable for the engraving process and will produce high-quality results. Here's a step-by-step guide on how to prepare vector graphics for laser engraving:

1. **Choose the Right Design Software:**

    - Start by using design software that allows you to create and edit vector graphics. Popular choices include Adobe Illustrator, CorelDRAW, Inkscape (a free and open-source option), and various CAD software for 3D engraving.

2. **Create or Import Your Design:**

    - Begin by creating your design from scratch or importing existing vector artwork into the design software. Vector graphics are composed of mathematical paths and shapes, which can be resized without loss of quality.

3. **Set the Document Size:**

    - Ensure that your document size in the design software matches the dimensions of the material you plan to engrave on. This step helps you visualize how the final engraving will fit on the material.

4. **Design Considerations:**

    - Pay attention to the design itself. Consider factors such as line thickness, shapes, curves, and the overall composition. Adjust these elements to achieve the desired look and feel for your engraving.

5. **Convert Text to Outlines:**

- If your design includes text, convert it to outlines (also called "paths" or "curves") to ensure that the font is preserved, and the text appears correctly when engraved. In Adobe Illustrator, you can do this by selecting the text and then choosing "Type" > "Create Outlines."

6. **Define Stroke and Fill Colors:**

   - Define the stroke (outline) and fill colors for your vector objects. The stroke defines the outline of shapes, and the fill defines the interior color. Use appropriate stroke and fill colors to indicate how you want the laser to engrave each element.

7. **Set Line Thickness and Properties:**

   - Adjust the line thickness (stroke width) for different elements in your design to control the engraving depth and emphasis. Thicker lines may result in deeper engravings.

8. **Combine or Group Elements:**

   - Organize your design by combining or grouping related elements. This helps maintain the design's integrity during the engraving process.

9. **Check for Overlapping Paths:**

   - Ensure that there are no overlapping or intersecting paths in your design, as this can cause issues during engraving. Use the "Pathfinder" tool or similar functions to merge overlapping shapes if necessary.

10. **Preview and Test:**

    - Use the preview feature in your design software to simulate how the engraving will look. If possible, run a test engraving on scrap material to verify that your design works as intended.

11. **Save in the Correct Format:**

    - Save your vector design in a format compatible with your laser engraving machine's software. Common file formats include SVG, AI, DXF, and EPS. Check your machine's documentation for specific format requirements.

12. **Clean Your Design:**

    - Before sending the design to the laser engraving machine, ensure that it's free of stray or unwanted paths, artifacts, or unnecessary elements that could affect the engraving quality.

13. **Export or Transfer the File:**

- Export or transfer the prepared vector file to the computer or software that controls your laser engraving machine. Follow the steps provided by your machine's manufacturer for this process.

14. **Set Laser Parameters:**

- In the laser engraving software, configure the laser parameters, including power, speed, and frequency, based on your material and design specifications.

15. **Position and Secure the Material:**

- Place the material to be engraved onto the engraving bed of your laser machine, ensuring it is securely positioned and level.

16. **Run the Engraving Job:**

- Start the engraving process according to the settings you configured in the laser engraving software.

By following these steps, you can prepare vector graphics for laser engraving effectively and ensure that your designs are well-suited for the engraving process, resulting in high-quality and accurate engravings.

Software and Tools for Design

Creating designs for laser engravings requires design software and tools that are capable of producing vector graphics. Vector graphics are essential because they can be scaled without losing quality and are well-suited for laser engraving. Here are some popular software and tools for designing laser engravings:

1. **Adobe Illustrator:**

- Adobe Illustrator is a professional vector graphics software widely used in the design industry. It offers a range of powerful tools for creating and editing vector-based designs. Illustrator is compatible with many laser engraving machines and is a top choice for laser engraving design.

2. **CorelDRAW:**

- CorelDRAW is another professional vector graphics software known for its versatility and user-friendly interface. It's suitable for creating detailed vector designs and is often used in laser engraving applications.

3. **Inkscape:**

- Inkscape is a free and open-source vector graphics software. It's a popular choice among hobbyists and budget-conscious users. Inkscape offers many features comparable to paid software options.

4. **AutoCAD:**

- AutoCAD is a CAD (Computer-Aided Design) software used primarily for architectural and engineering applications. It's suitable for creating precise vector-based designs, especially for 3D engraving.

5. **Rhino (Rhinoceros):**

   - Rhino is a 3D modeling software known for its versatility in creating 3D designs. It's often used for 3D engraving projects that require complex geometries.

6. **Gravit Designer:**

   - Gravit Designer is a web-based vector design tool that offers both free and paid versions. It's user-friendly and accessible from any device with an internet connection.

7. **Vectr:**

   - Vectr is another free web-based vector graphics tool that's easy to use and suitable for creating simple designs for laser engraving.

8. **CAD Software (e.g., SolidWorks, Fusion 360):**

   - CAD software is excellent for creating intricate 3D designs and mechanical parts. CAD designs can be imported into other software for further customization or directly into laser engraving machines.

9. **3D Modeling Software (e.g., Blender, Tinkercad):**

   - For 3D engraving projects, consider 3D modeling software that can create 3D designs or convert 2D designs into 3D format.

10. **Online Design Marketplaces:**

    - Online design marketplaces like Shutterstock, Adobe Stock, and Etsy offer a vast library of vector graphics, illustrations, and templates that you can purchase and use for laser engraving projects. Be sure to check licensing terms and permissions for commercial use.

11. **Graphic Tablets and Stylus Tools:**

    - If you prefer drawing by hand, graphic tablets such as Wacom and stylus tools can be used in conjunction with vector design software to create custom drawings and designs

When choosing design software, consider factors such as your level of experience, budget, the complexity of your projects, and compatibility with your laser engraving machine. Most laser engraving machines come with their software, so make sure to check the software options provided by the manufacturer and ensure they are compatible with your design needs.

Tips for Designing Engraving-Friendly Artwork

Designing artwork that is laser engraving friendly is crucial to achieving high-quality and precise engravings. Here are some tips to help you create designs that work well with laser engraving:

1. **Use Vector Graphics:** Vector graphics are essential for laser engraving because they maintain sharpness and clarity at any size. Design your artwork using vector-based software like Adobe Illustrator or CorelDRAW.

2. **Consider Material Compatibility:** Different materials require different settings for laser engraving. Before designing, know the material you'll be engraving on and research its specific engraving requirements.

3. **Design in Black and White:** Start your design in black and white or grayscale. Laser engraving works by varying the depth or intensity of the engraved area, so a monochromatic design provides better control over engraving effects.

4. **Define Stroke Width:** When using lines or strokes in your design, ensure that the stroke width is appropriate for your desired engraving depth. Thicker lines will result in deeper engravings.

5. **Choose the Right Fonts:** Select fonts that are clear and legible at the desired size. Avoid overly intricate or decorative fonts that may not engrave well. Convert text to outlines to ensure font compatibility.

6. **Contrast is Key:** Create clear contrast between the design and the background. High contrast makes the engraving stand out and enhances visibility.

7. **Test Your Design:** Before engraving on your final material, run test engravings on scrap pieces to fine-tune settings and ensure the design appears as intended.

8. **Watch for Fine Details:** Be cautious with very fine details or small text, especially when engraving on textured or irregular surfaces. Fine details may not be visible or may not be engraved well.

9. **Raster Images:** If including raster images (like photographs), use high-resolution images for best results. Keep in mind that photos may need to be converted to grayscale or halftone for engraving.

10. **Check for Overlapping Elements:** Ensure that there are no overlapping or intersecting elements in your design, as these can cause unexpected results during engraving. Use software tools to combine or trim shapes as needed.

11. **Safety Text and Symbols:** If engraving safety information or warning symbols, make sure they are clear and comply with safety standards.

12. **Simplify Complex Designs:** Complex designs with many small elements may take a long time to engrave and can result in intricate patterns that may not be visible at a glance. Simplify complex designs to achieve cleaner results.

13. **Adjust Speed and Power:** Experiment with engraving speed and laser power settings to achieve the desired depth and contrast in your design. Be prepared to adjust settings for different materials.

14. **Use a Preview Feature:** Most laser engraving software offers a preview feature that allows you to visualize how the design will appear on the material. Use this feature to make any necessary adjustments before engraving.

15. **Documentation and Notes:** Keep a record of your design settings and any adjustments made during the engraving process. This documentation can be valuable for replicating successful results in the future.

By following these tips and considering the specific requirements of your laser engraving project, you can create artwork that is laser engraving friendly and produces excellent results.

Chapter 5: Laser Engraving Techniques

Laser engraving techniques encompass various methods and approaches to achieve different effects and results when using a laser engraving machine. These techniques can be employed to create different textures, depths, and visual effects in the engraved material. Here are some common laser engraving techniques:

1. **Raster Engraving:**

   - Raster engraving is the standard technique used for engraving images, text, and detailed designs. It involves the laser moving back and forth across the material while varying the laser power and speed. This technique can create varying shades of gray and simulate grayscale images by varying the density of engraved dots.

2. **Vector Cutting:**

   - Vector cutting, also known as vector engraving, involves the use of vector paths or lines to cut through the material entirely. This technique is often used for creating precise cutouts, shapes, or intricate designs in addition to engraving.

3. **Line Engraving:**

   - Line engraving is a technique where the laser follows a specific path to engrave fine lines or patterns. This technique is commonly used for decorative purposes, such as creating intricate linework, patterns, or borders.

4. **Halftone Engraving:**

   - Halftone engraving involves converting grayscale images into patterns of varying dot sizes. This technique is used to simulate shades of gray or create gradients in the engraving. It can add depth and texture to the engraving.

5. **3D Engraving:**

   - 3D engraving, also known as 3D relief engraving, involves the laser varying its power and focus to create depth in the engraved material. This technique is used for sculptural or three-dimensional effects, such as engraving on uneven or contoured surfaces.

6. **Ablation Engraving:**

   - Ablation engraving is a technique where the laser removes material to create engraved areas. It's often used for marking and serial numbers on metals or other materials. The laser's power and duration are controlled to achieve precise depth and quality.

7. **Inlay Engraving:**

   - Inlay engraving involves engraving a design or text into a material and then filling the engraved area with a contrasting material. This technique creates visually striking engravings with color contrast.

8. **Ceramic and Glass Engraving:**

- Engraving on ceramics and glass requires special techniques and often involves using lasers with shorter wavelengths, such as UV lasers. These lasers create fine, intricate engravings on these materials.

9. **Color Filling:**

- Color filling is a technique where engraved areas are filled with paint or other materials to add color and contrast to the design. This technique is commonly used for signage and decorative items.

10. **Reverse Engraving:**

- Reverse engraving involves engraving on the backside of transparent or translucent materials, such as acrylic or glass. When viewed from the front, the engraved areas appear raised and create a 3D effect.

11. **Texture Engraving:**

- Texture engraving is a technique used to create tactile textures on the surface of materials. This can be used for decorative purposes or to enhance the grip and feel of products.

12. **Deep Engraving:**

- Deep engraving involves using high laser power and slow speeds to create deep, pronounced engravings. This technique is suitable for applications where depth is a primary consideration.

The choice of technique depends on the material, the desired effect, and the specific application. Experimentation and familiarity with your laser engraving machine and software are often necessary to achieve the desired results.

Focusing Your Laser

Focusing a laser engraver is a crucial step to ensure precise and high-quality results. Here's a step-by-step guide on how to focus your laser engraver:

Note: The exact steps and tools required for focusing may vary depending on the make and model of your laser engraving machine. Consult your machine's user manual for specific instructions tailored to your equipment.

1. **Safety Precautions:**

- Before you begin, ensure that you are wearing the necessary laser safety goggles and that all safety interlocks on your laser engraver are functioning correctly.

2. **Prepare the Material:**

- Place the material you intend to engrave or cut onto the engraving bed. Ensure that it securely fastened, level, and properly aligned.

3. **Clean the Lens:**

- Check the focusing lens for any dust, debris, or smudges. Clean it using lens cleaning supplies designed for laser optics to avoid damaging the lens.

4. **Adjust the Z-Axis:**

- If your laser engraving machine has a motorized Z-axis or manual focus adjustment, use it to position the laser head at the approximate focal point. This point is typically just above the material's surface.

5. **Focus Tool or Material Test:**

- Many laser engraving machines come with a focus tool or a test piece of material with a calibrated surface to aid in focusing. If available, use these tools as they simplify the process.

6. **Manual Focusing:**

- If you need to manually focus the laser, follow these steps: a. Place a piece of material identical to the one you'll be engraving or cutting onto the engraving bed. b. Start with the Z-axis slightly above the material's surface. c. Slowly lower the Z-axis while observing the laser dot or beam through the laser viewing window. d. The goal is to find the point where the laser beam is the smallest and most concentrated.

7. **Check for Consistency:**

- Move the laser head to different locations on the material to ensure that the focal point remains consistent across the entire engraving area. Make Z-axis adjustments as needed to maintain focus.

8. **Test Engraving:**

- Before starting your full engraving or cutting job, perform a small test engraving on the material. Examine the engraving quality and depth to verify that the focus is correct.

9. **Record Settings:**

- Once you've determined the correct focal point, record the Z-axis or focus settings for future reference. This is particularly important if you plan to work with the same material and lens in the future.

10. **Repeat as Needed:**

- If you change materials or lenses, repeat the focusing process to ensure that you achieve optimal results for each specific setup.

Properly focusing your laser engraver is essential for achieving precise and consistent engraving or cutting results. It may take some practice to become proficient at this skill, but it is a critical step in the laser engraving process.

Setting Speed and Power

Setting the speed and power of your laser engraver is essential to achieve the desired results for your specific engraving or cutting job. The optimal settings depend on factors such as the material being processed, the design complexity, and the laser power available on your machine. Here's a step-by-step guide on how to set the speed and power for your laser engraver:

1. **Material Selection:**

   - Choose the material you'll be working with, and ensure it is suitable for laser engraving or cutting. Different materials have unique requirements for speed and power settings.

2. **Refer to Material Guidelines:**

   - Consult the material guidelines provided by the manufacturer of your laser engraver or the material supplier. These guidelines often include recommended speed and power settings for various materials.

3. **Material Testing:**

   - If you are working with a material for the first time or if the guidelines are unavailable, it's essential to perform material tests. Cut or engrave small test pieces of the material using various speed and power combinations to determine the best settings.

4. **Adjust the Speed:**

   - Start by adjusting the engraving or cutting speed. Slower speeds typically result in deeper engravings or cuts, while faster speeds produce shallower engravings or cuts. You may need to find a balance between speed and quality.

5. **Adjust the Power:**

   - Adjust the laser power setting to control the intensity of the laser beam. Higher power levels create deeper engravings or faster cuts, while lower power levels create shallower engravings or slower cuts. Finding the right power level is crucial for achieving the desired effect.

6. **Raster and Vector Settings:**

   - Different elements within your design may require different settings. For example, you can adjust the speed and power settings separately for raster engraving (fills, shading) and vector cutting (lines, outlines). Configure these settings in your laser engraving software.

7. **Consider Scan Gap or Dots Per Inch (DPI):**

- Adjust the scan gap or DPI settings in your laser engraving software. A higher DPI results in finer details and may require slower speeds. Conversely, a lower DPI may allow for faster engraving with less detail.

8. **Test Engraving:**

- Before proceeding with the full engraving or cutting job, perform a test engraving or cut on a scrap piece of the material. This allows you to verify that the settings are appropriate and achieve the desired outcome.

9. **Keep Notes:**

- Record the optimal speed and power settings for each material and specific job. This documentation will be valuable for future projects and can help you avoid repeating the testing process.

10. **Monitor the Process:**

- While the laser engraving or cutting job is in progress, monitor the machine closely to ensure that the settings are producing the desired results. Make adjustments if necessary.

11. **Safety Precautions:**

- Always adhere to safety precautions when working with laser equipment. Wear appropriate laser safety goggles and ensure that the laser machine's safety interlocks are functioning correctly.

12. **Document Settings for Reproducibility:**

- For repeat jobs or future projects with similar materials, refer to your documented settings to achieve consistent results.

Achieving the correct speed and power settings for your laser engraver may require some trial and error, especially when working with new materials or intricate designs. Careful testing and adjustment are key to achieving the best possible results.

Engraving Depth and Resolution

Engraving depth and resolution are two critical aspects of laser engraving that determine the quality and appearance of the result. Here's an explanation of each and how they are interrelated:

1. **Engraving Depth:**

- Engraving depth refers to how deep the laser beam penetrates the material during the engraving process. It is typically measured in units such as millimeters (mm) or inches (in).
- Factors Affecting Engraving Depth:

- **Laser Power:** Higher laser power can create deeper engravings.

- **Engraving Speed:** Slower engraving speeds allow the laser more time to remove material, resulting in deeper engravings.

- **Material Type:** Different materials have varying engraving depths based on their hardness, density, and composition.

- **Focus:** Properly focusing the laser can affect the depth of the engraving.

- **Number of Passes:** Running multiple passes over the same area can increase the engraving depth.

- Use Cases:

  - Engraving depth is essential when creating tactile or 3D effects, such as embossed designs or sculptural engravings.

  - For applications like cutting or marking, engraving depth may be less critical compared to engraving intricate patterns or designs.

2. **Resolution:**

   - Resolution in laser engraving refers to the level of detail and precision in the engraving. It is measured in dots per inch (DPI) or lines per inch (LPI) and represents the number of individual laser dots or lines within a specific area.

   - Factors Affecting Resolution:

     - **DPI/LPI Setting:** The higher the DPI/LPI setting, the finer the level of detail in the engraving.

     - **Engraving Speed:** Slower speeds can allow for finer details and higher resolution.

     - **Material Properties:** The material's surface and composition can influence the achievable resolution.

   - Use Cases:

     - High-resolution engravings are necessary for intricate designs, fine text, and detailed artwork.

     - Lower resolution may be acceptable for applications where fine detail is not a primary concern, such as industrial part marking.

Interrelation Between Depth and Resolution:

- Engraving depth and resolution are interrelated because changing one parameter can affect the other. For example:

- Increasing the laser power and slowing down the engraving speed may result in deeper engravings but could reduce resolution if the laser beam interacts with the material for an extended period, causing melting or charring.

- Using a high-resolution setting may create fine details, but it could result in shallow engravings if the laser power and speed settings are not adjusted to allow for sufficient material removal.

- Achieving the right balance between engraving depth and resolution is crucial to producing the desired outcome for a specific project. It often requires experimentation and testing with different settings to find the optimal combination.

- Some laser engraving machines allow you to control both depth and resolution independently, providing flexibility for a wide range of applications. Understanding the material's characteristics and the goals of your project will guide your choices when adjusting these parameters for laser engraving.

Techniques for Different Materials

Laser engraving techniques can vary significantly depending on the type of material you are working with. Each material has unique properties, and selecting the appropriate technique is essential for achieving the desired results. Here are some laser engraving techniques for different materials:

1. **Wood:**
   - **Raster Engraving:** Wood engraves beautifully with raster engraving, allowing for detailed patterns, text, and images. Adjust the speed and power settings to control depth and shading.
   - **Vector Cutting:** For cutting wooden materials, use vector cutting to create precise shapes and intricate designs.
   - **3D Engraving:** Wood can be 3D engraved to create sculptural effects and depth. Experiment with varying power and speed settings to achieve different levels of relief.

2. **Acrylic:**
   - **Raster Engraving:** Acrylic is commonly used for creating signage and decorative items. Raster engraving provides precise and detailed results. Adjust the speed and power settings for the desired engraving depth.
   - **Vector Cutting:** Vector cutting is ideal for producing clean, polished edges when cutting acrylic sheets. Use it for creating shapes, letters, or logos.
   - **Reverse Engraving:** Engrave on the backside of acrylic to create a 3D, raised effect on the front side.

3. **Glass:**

- **Ablation Engraving:** Glass can be engraved using ablation, which removes a portion of the material's surface. Achieve varying levels of opacity by adjusting laser power and speed.
- **Color Filling:** After engraving, apply color to the engraved areas to create contrasting and decorative effects.

4. **Metal:**

- **Annealing:** Metal engraving can be done using annealing techniques, which heat the metal to create a color change without cutting or removing material. Adjust power and speed to control the color and depth.
- **Ablation Engraving:** For deeper metal engraving or cutting, use ablation techniques, which remove material. Laser power and speed settings must be carefully adjusted based on the metal's type and thickness.

5. **Leather:**

- **Raster Engraving:** Leather engraving can create intricate patterns and designs. Adjust the settings to control engraving depth and shading.
- **Color Filling:** After engraving, color fill the engraved areas to add contrast and highlight the design.

6. **Plastic:**

- **Raster Engraving:** Plastics can be engraved with raster techniques. Experiment with different settings for depth and detail.
- **Vector Cutting:** Use vector cutting for cleanly cutting plastic sheets into specific shapes or parts.

7. **Stone and Tile:**

- **Ablation Engraving:** Stone and tile can be engraved by removing the top layer of material using ablation techniques. Adjust power and speed for desired results.
- **3D Engraving:** Create depth and texture on stone surfaces using 3D engraving techniques for decorative applications.

8. **Paper and Cardboard:**

- **Raster Engraving:** Raster engraving can be used to create intricate paper or cardboard designs. Adjust settings for the desired depth of engraving.
- **Vector Cutting:** Use vector cutting for precision when cutting paper or cardboard into specific shapes or designs.

9. **Textiles:**

- **Raster Engraving:** Engrave on textiles to create patterns, logos, or designs. Adjust settings for different engraving depths.

- **Color Filling:** After engraving, add color to the engraved areas for contrast and vibrancy.

10. **Ceramic and Porcelain:**

- **Ablation Engraving:** Engrave on ceramic or porcelain by removing the top layer using ablation techniques. Experiment with settings for depth and detail.

These are general techniques for various materials, but the optimal settings and approaches may vary based on the specific type and brand of material you are using, as well as the capabilities of your laser engraving machine. Always perform test engravings on a small piece of the material to determine the best settings for your project.

Chapter 6: Operating Your Laser Engraver

Operating a laser engraver requires careful attention to safety, as well as a good understanding of the machine's controls and software. Here's a step-by-step guide on how to operate your laser engraver:

Note: Specific instructions may vary depending on the make and model of your laser engraving machine, so always refer to your machine's user manual for detailed guidelines and safety precautions.

1. **Safety Precautions:**

- Before you begin, ensure you have the appropriate laser safety goggles for your machine's wavelength. Laser safety is paramount.

- Confirm that emergency stop buttons and safety interlocks are functioning correctly.

- Remove any flammable materials or hazards from the working area.

2. **Power On the Machine:**

- Turn on the power to your laser engraver and ensure all systems are initializing properly.

3. **Material Preparation:**

- Place the material you intend to engrave or cut onto the engraving bed. Ensure it's securely fastened, level, and properly aligned.

4. **Set Up the Computer:**

- Prepare the computer connected to the laser engraver.

- Install and open the laser engraving software provided by the manufacturer.

- Import or create your design within the software.

5. **Configure Laser Settings:**

- Configure the laser settings within the software, including power, speed, frequency, and any other relevant parameters.
- Choose the appropriate engraving mode (raster or vector) for your design.

6. **Calibrate the Focusing:**

- Focus the laser beam for the material you are using. Adjust the Z-axis to achieve the correct focal point.
- Use a focus tool or perform manual focusing, as described in previous responses.

7. **Preview and Set Origin:**

- Use the laser engraving software to preview the engraving path to ensure it aligns with your material.
- Set the starting point (origin) for the engraving on your material using the software's controls.

8. **Run a Test Engraving:**

- Before proceeding with the full engraving or cutting job, run a test engraving on a scrap piece of the material. Check the engraving quality, depth, and alignment to ensure your settings are correct.

9. **Start the Engraving Process:**

- Once you are satisfied with the test engraving, start the full engraving process using the software's controls.
- Monitor the engraving to ensure it proceeds as expected. Be ready to pause or stop the process if any issues arise.

10. **Post-Processing:**

- After the engraving is complete, carefully remove the engraved material from the engraving bed.
- If necessary, clean the engraved material to remove any residue or debris.

11. **Shutdown and Maintenance:**

- Turn off the laser engraver and the computer.
- Clean the engraving bed, lens, and surrounding area to maintain machine performance.
- Follow any additional maintenance procedures specified in your machine's user manual

12. **Record Settings:**

- Document the settings you used for the job, including laser power, speed, focus, and any other relevant parameters. This record can be helpful for future projects.

13. **Safety Always Comes First:**

- Always prioritize safety when operating a laser engraver. Follow all safety guidelines and precautions provided by the manufacturer and be vigilant throughout the entire process.

Operating a laser engraver requires practice and experience to achieve the best results. Familiarize yourself with your specific machine, experiment with different settings, and continue to refine your skills to produce high-quality laser engravings.

Loading Materials

Loading materials into your laser engraving machine is an essential step in the engraving or cutting process. Proper material placement and alignment ensure accurate results and prevent damage to the machine. Here's how to load materials into your laser engraver:

Note: The following steps are general guidelines, and the exact process may vary depending on the make and model of your laser engraving machine. Always consult your machine's user manual for specific instructions.

1. **Safety Precautions:**

   - Before you begin, ensure you are wearing appropriate laser safety goggles and that all safety interlocks on the laser engraver are functioning correctly.

2. **Prepare the Material:**

   - Place the material you intend to engrave or cut onto a clean, flat, and level surface. Ensure the material is free from dust, dirt, or debris.

3. **Material Size and Alignment:**

   - Measure and cut your material to the appropriate size for the engraving or cutting job.

   - Align the material with the engraving bed's edges to ensure it is square and parallel. Use guides or rulers if available.

4. **Material Thickness:**

   - Adjust the Z-axis or bed height to accommodate the thickness of the material. Most laser engraving machines have a movable bed or Z-axis that can be adjusted to accommodate materials of different thicknesses.

5. **Material Fastening:**

   - Securely fasten the material to the engraving bed to prevent movement during the engraving or cutting process. Common methods include:

- Masking tape or painter's tape: Use tape to secure the material to the bed's surface. Ensure it is taut and wrinkle-free.

- Vacuum table or hold-down clamps: Some laser engravers come with vacuum tables or clamps to securely hold materials in place.

- Honeycomb bed: If your machine has a honeycomb bed, place your material on top of it for support.

6. **Set the Origin Point:**

   - Use the laser engraving software to set the origin point (starting position) for the engraving or cutting job. This ensures that the laser head begins its operation in the correct location on the material.

7. **Preview the Job:**

   - Preview the engraving or cutting path within the laser engraving software to confirm that the design aligns correctly with the material. Make any necessary adjustments if the alignment is off.

8. **Safety Check:**

   - Double-check all safety measures, including laser safety goggles, proper ventilation, and the machine's safety interlocks.

9. **Start the Job:**

   - Start the laser engraving or cutting process using the controls within the software. The laser head will follow the designated path and engrave or cut the material according to your design.

10. **Monitor the Process:**

    - Continuously monitor the engraving or cutting process to ensure that it proceeds as expected. Be prepared to pause or stop the process if any issues arise.

11. **Unload the Material:**

    - Once the engraving or cutting is complete, carefully remove the material from the engraving bed. Ensure that it is free from any residue or debris.

12. **Shutdown and Maintenance:**

    - Turn off the laser engraver and the computer.

    - Clean the engraving bed, lens, and surrounding area to maintain machine performance.

- Follow any additional maintenance procedures specified in your machine's user manual.

Properly loading materials into your laser engraving machine is crucial for achieving accurate and high-quality results. Take your time to align and secure the material correctly, and always prioritize safety when working with laser equipment.

Starting the Engraving Process

Starting the engraving process on a laser engraving machine involves several steps, from setting up your design to executing the job. Here's a step-by-step guide on how to start the engraving process:

Note: These instructions are general guidelines, and the specific steps may vary depending on the make and model of your laser engraving machine and the software you are using. Always consult your machine's user manual for detailed instructions tailored to your equipment.

1. **Design Preparation:**

   - Create or import the design you want to engrave into your laser engraving software. Ensure that the design is properly sized and positioned on the virtual workspace.

2. **Configure Laser Settings:**

   - Configure the laser settings within the software, including power, speed, frequency (if applicable), and any other relevant parameters.
   - Choose the appropriate engraving mode (raster or vector) for your design.

3. **Calibrate the Focusing:**

   - Focus the laser beam for the material you are using. Adjust the Z-axis to achieve the correct focal point. Use a focus tool or perform manual focusing, as needed.

4. **Preview the Job:**

   - Use the laser engraving software to preview the engraving path to ensure it aligns with your material and design.
   - Verify that the origin point (starting position) is correctly set for the engraving.

5. **Material Preparation:**

   - Place the material you intend to engrave on the engraving bed. Ensure it is securely fastened, level, and properly aligned. Adjust the Z-axis or bed height to accommodate the material's thickness.

6. **Safety Precautions:**

   - Before you start the engraving process, ensure you are wearing the appropriate laser safety goggles for your machine's wavelength.
   - Confirm that emergency stop buttons and safety interlocks on the laser engraver are functioning correctly.

- Remove any flammable materials or hazards from the working area.

7. **Set the Origin Point:**

   - Double-check that the origin point (starting position) is accurately set within the software to ensure that the laser head begins its operation in the correct location on the material.

8. **Safety Check:**

   - Double-check all safety measures, including laser safety goggles, proper ventilation, and the machine's safety interlocks.

9. **Start the Engraving Process:**

   - Once you are satisfied with the design, settings, and material placement, initiate the engraving process using the controls provided by the laser engraving software. The laser head will follow the designated path and engrave the material according to your design.

10. **Monitor the Process:**

    - Continuously monitor the engraving process to ensure that it proceeds as expected. Be prepared to pause or stop the process if any issues arise or if you need to make real-time adjustments.

11. **Post-Processing:**

    - After the engraving is complete, carefully remove the engraved material from the engraving bed. Ensure that it is free from any residue or debris.

12. **Shutdown and Maintenance:**

    - Turn off the laser engraver and the computer.

    - Clean the engraving bed, lens, and surrounding area to maintain machine performance.

    - Follow any additional maintenance procedures specified in your machine's user manual.

Starting the engraving process requires attention to detail, safety precautions, and a thorough understanding of your laser engraving machine and software. With practice, you can achieve accurate and high-quality engraving results for a wide range of applications.

Troubleshooting Common Issues

Troubleshooting common laser engraving setup errors is essential to ensure that your engraving projects proceed smoothly. Here are some common setup errors and their solutions:

1. **Incorrect Material Placement:**

   - Error: The material is not correctly aligned, leveled, or securely fastened on the engraving bed.

- Solution: Check that the material is properly positioned, level, and securely fastened to prevent movement during the engraving process.

2. **Incorrect Focusing:**

   - Error: The laser beam is not correctly focused on the material's surface, resulting in blurry or shallow engravings.

   - Solution: Recheck the focusing by adjusting the Z-axis or focus settings to achieve the correct focal point for the material.

3. **Wrong Speed and Power Settings:**

   - Error: Inaccurate speed and power settings can lead to under-engraving, over-engraving, or charring of the material.

   - Solution: Consult material guidelines or perform test engravings to determine the optimal speed and power settings for the specific material you are using.

4. **Alignment Issues:**

   - Error: The engraving is not aligned with the material correctly, resulting in off-center or misaligned engravings.

   - Solution: Ensure that the origin point is set accurately within the software and that the material is positioned to align with the engraving design.

5. **Laser Head Obstruction:**

   - Error: The laser head or lens may be obstructed by debris or residue, affecting engraving quality.

   - Solution: Check and clean the laser head and lens to remove any debris, residue, or obstructions that may be affecting the laser's performance.

6. **Software Issues:**

   - Error: Problems with the engraving software, such as design import errors or software crashes.

   - Solution: Restart the software and computer. Ensure that your design files are in a compatible format and free from errors. Update your software to the latest version if available.

7. **Inadequate Ventilation:**

   - Error: Poor ventilation can lead to smoke and fumes buildup, which can affect engraving quality and safety.

- Solution: Ensure that your engraving area has proper ventilation and exhaust systems to remove smoke and fumes. Replace or clean air filters as needed.

8. **Laser Safety Precautions:**

   - Error: Failure to follow laser safety protocols can lead to potential hazards.

   - Solution: Always wear appropriate laser safety goggles, adhere to safety interlocks, and follow recommended safety guidelines when working with laser equipment.

9. **Material Compatibility:**

   - Error: Attempting to engrave materials that are not suitable for laser engraving can result in damage or poor results.

   - Solution: Verify that the material you are using is compatible with laser engraving and cutting processes. Consult material guidelines to ensure suitability.

10. **Hardware Malfunctions:**

    - Error: Technical issues or malfunctions with the laser engraving machine.

    - Solution: If you encounter consistent problems despite troubleshooting, contact your machine's manufacturer or service provider for technical support and repairs.

11. **Inadequate Cleaning and Maintenance:**

    - Error: Neglecting regular cleaning and maintenance can lead to performance issues over time.

    - Solution: Follow the recommended cleaning and maintenance schedule outlined in your machine's user manual to ensure optimal performance and longevity.

By identifying and addressing these common setup errors, you can improve the accuracy and quality of your laser engraving projects and maintain the safety and functionality of your laser engraving machine.

Maintenance and Cleaning

Proper maintenance and cleaning of your laser engraving machine are crucial for ensuring its longevity, optimal performance, and safety. Regular maintenance helps prevent issues and extends the lifespan of the equipment. Here's a guide on how to maintain and clean your laser machine:

Note: Always consult your machine's user manual for specific maintenance instructions, as procedures may vary depending on the make and model of your laser engraving machine.

General Maintenance:

1. **Safety Precautions:**
   - Before performing any maintenance, ensure that the machine is turned off and that the power source is disconnected. Follow appropriate lockout/tagout procedures.

2. **Cleaning:**
   - Regularly clean the exterior surfaces of the machine using a soft, lint-free cloth or sponge. Use a mild, non-abrasive cleaning solution if needed, but avoid harsh chemicals that may damage the machine's finish.

3. **Ventilation System:**
   - Inspect and clean the ventilation system, including fans and filters, to ensure proper airflow. Replace or clean air filters as recommended by the manufacturer to maintain efficient smoke and fume extraction.

4. **Laser Optics and Lens:**
   - Clean the laser lens and optics using a lint-free, laser-safe cleaning cloth and a specialized lens cleaning solution. Handle the lens with care to avoid scratches.

5. **Rails and Bearings:**
   - Lubricate the machine's rails and linear bearings as specified in the user manual. Use the recommended lubricant to prevent excessive wear and maintain smooth motion.

6. **Belts and Pulleys:**
   - Check the condition of belts and pulleys and tighten or replace them if necessary. Ensure proper tension for accurate engraving and cutting.

7. **Laser Tube:**
   - Inspect the condition of the laser tube and associated components. If you notice damage or signs of wear, consult a technician for repairs or replacements.

8. **Cooling System:**
   - Maintain the cooling system, including the water reservoir and pump, to prevent overheating of the laser tube. Keep the cooling water clean and at the appropriate temperature.

9. **Electrical Connections:**
   - Periodically inspect electrical connections, wires, and cables for signs of wear, damage, or loose connections. Ensure that all connections are secure and free from debris.

Routine Cleaning After Each Use:

1. **Engraving Bed:**

- Clean the engraving bed after each use to remove any residue, debris, or leftover material. Use a brush, air compressor, or a vacuum system to clear the bed.

2. **Laser Head and Nozzles:**

   - Remove and clean the laser head and nozzle to ensure they are free from debris and residue. Check for any obstructions in the laser head's path.

Weekly or Biweekly Maintenance:

1. **Optical Alignment:**

   - Periodically check and adjust the optical alignment if necessary to ensure accurate engraving and cutting results.

2. **Focus Adjustment:**

   - Recheck and adjust the focus as needed to maintain the optimal focal point for different materials.

3. **Testing:**

   - Run a test job to ensure that the laser engraving machine is operating correctly and producing the desired results.

Quarterly Maintenance:

1. **Inspect and Replace Consumables:**

   - Check and replace consumable parts such as laser tubes, mirrors, and lenses if they are reaching the end of their service life or show signs of degradation.

Annual Maintenance:

1. **Professional Service:**

   - Arrange for professional servicing of your laser engraving machine at least once a year. A qualified technician can perform a comprehensive inspection and maintenance to address any issues and ensure the machine's longevity.

Remember that proper maintenance is essential for safety, consistent performance, and the quality of your laser engraving projects. By following these maintenance guidelines and scheduling regular check-ups, you can keep your laser engraving machine in top condition.

Chapter 7: Safety and Maintenance

Laser Safety Guidelines

Laser safety is of paramount importance when working with laser engraving machines, as lasers can pose significant risks to human health and safety if not handled properly. Here are essential laser safety guidelines to follow:

1. Wear Appropriate Laser Safety Goggles:

- Always wear laser safety goggles specifically designed for the laser's wavelength when operating the machine. These goggles protect your eyes from direct and scattered laser light.

2. Control Access:

- Restrict access to the laser engraving area to authorized personnel only. Ensure that untrained individuals, especially children, are kept away from the machine.

3. Laser Interlocks:

- Ensure that all safety interlock systems on the laser engraver are functioning correctly. These interlocks should prevent the laser from operating when doors or panels are open.

4. Emergency Stop:

- Familiarize yourself with the location and operation of the emergency stop button on the laser engraving machine. Be ready to use it in case of any unexpected emergencies or issues.

5. Ventilation and Extraction:

- Maintain proper ventilation and fume extraction to remove smoke, fumes, and particulates generated during the engraving or cutting process. Ensure that the exhaust system is functioning correctly.

6. Material Compatibility:

- Only use materials that are approved for laser engraving in your machine. Using unsuitable materials can result in hazardous reactions or emissions.

7. Fire Safety:

- Have fire safety equipment, such as fire extinguishers, nearby and ready for use. Laser engraving can generate heat, and fires are a potential risk.

8. Material Precautions:

- Be aware of the materials you are engraving. Some materials, like PVC or materials containing chlorine, can release toxic gases when exposed to lasers.

9. No Reflective Surfaces:

- Avoid using or engraving reflective materials, as they can bounce the laser beam unpredictably and cause harm.

10. Eye Protection for Others: - Ensure that bystanders and anyone in the vicinity of the laser engraving area wear appropriate laser safety goggles or are shielded from direct laser light.

11. Training: - Ensure that anyone operating the laser engraving machine has received proper training on its safe operation, including laser safety protocols and emergency procedures.

12. Regular Maintenance: - Perform routine maintenance and cleaning of the laser engraving machine to keep it in safe working condition.

13. Laser Classification and Labeling: - Ensure that your laser engraving machine is properly classified and labeled based on its power and wavelength according to international standards (e.g., ANSI Z136.1 in the United States).

14. Warning Labels: - Maintain warning labels on the machine that indicate the laser's class, wavelength, and hazards. Do not remove or deface these labels.

15. Proper Setup and Calibration: - Follow manufacturer guidelines for setting up and calibrating your laser engraving machine. Improper setup can result in unintended laser exposure.

16. Record Keeping: - Keep records of maintenance, safety inspections, and any incidents or near misses related to laser use. Documentation can be valuable for safety audits and compliance.

17. Emergency Procedures: - Establish and communicate clear emergency procedures for laser related accidents, including injury, fire, or equipment malfunction.

18. Regulatory Compliance: - Comply with all local, national, and international regulations and standards related to laser safety.

19. Continuous Monitoring: - Continuously monitor the laser engraving process to ensure safety measures are in place and functioning correctly.

Laser safety is a shared responsibility among operators, supervisors, and equipment manufacturers. By following these guidelines and exercising vigilance, you can reduce the risks associated with laser engraving and ensure a safe working environment.

Proper Ventilation

Proper ventilation is crucial when operating a laser engraving machine to remove potentially harmful fumes, smoke, and particulates generated during the engraving or cutting process. Effective ventilation helps maintain a safe and healthy work environment. Here are guidelines for ensuring proper laser ventilation:

1. Exhaust System:

- Ensure that your laser engraving machine is equipped with a functioning exhaust or ventilation system. This system should consist of an exhaust fan or blower, ducting, and an exhaust outlet.

2. Location:

- Position the laser engraving machine in a well-ventilated area. It's ideal to place it near an exterior wall or window to allow for the easy installation of ducting.

3. Ducting:

- Use high-quality, non-flammable ducting that is resistant to chemical corrosion. The ducting should be properly sealed to prevent leaks.

4. Exhaust Outlet:

- The exhaust duct should lead to an outdoor exhaust outlet, not into a confined or shared workspace. Ensure that the exhaust outlet is properly directed away from windows, doors, or air intakes to prevent recirculation of fumes back into the workspace.

5. Airflow Direction:

- Establish a unidirectional airflow system where air is pulled away from the laser engraving machine and exhausted outdoors.

6. Airflow Rate:

- Size the exhaust fan or blower appropriately for your laser engraving machine and the materials you are working with. Consult the machine's specifications and follow manufacturer recommendations for airflow rates.

7. Filters:

- Consider installing additional filters, such as activated carbon filters or HEPA filters, to further purify the exhaust air and remove harmful contaminants.

8. Regular Maintenance:

- Perform regular maintenance on the ventilation system, including cleaning or replacing filters, checking ducts for blockages, and ensuring that the exhaust fan or blower is in good working condition.

9. Monitoring:

- Implement air quality monitoring to assess the effectiveness of the ventilation system and ensure that it is adequately removing fumes and particulates.

10. Personal Protective Equipment (PPE): - In addition to proper ventilation, provide laser safety goggles to protect against potential laser beam reflections or direct exposure.

11. Material Compatibility: - Be aware of the materials you are engraving, as some materials can release toxic fumes when exposed to laser energy. Ensure your ventilation system is equipped to handle the specific materials you use.

12. Safety Precautions: - Develop and communicate clear safety protocols regarding ventilation, including emergency procedures in case of ventilation system failures or other incidents.

13. Regulatory Compliance: - Ensure that your ventilation system complies with local, national, and international regulations and standards for air quality and workplace safety.

Proper laser ventilation not only protects the health and safety of personnel but also extends the lifespan of your laser engraving machine by reducing the risk of damage from smoke and fumes. Regularly inspect, maintain, and test your ventilation system to ensure it functions optimally during laser engraving operations.

Cleaning and Lens Maintenance

Cleaning and maintaining the laser lens and mirrors in your laser engraving machine is essential for achieving high-quality engraving and cutting results. Dust, debris, and residue can accumulate on these optical components over time, degrading performance. Here's a step-by-step guide on how to clean and maintain laser lenses and mirrors:

Note: Always follow the specific instructions provided in your laser engraving machine's user manual for lens and mirror maintenance, as procedures may vary depending on the machine's design and manufacturer recommendations.

Tools and Materials Needed:

1. **Lint-free laser-safe cleaning cloths:** Use cloths specifically designed for cleaning optical components to avoid scratching or damaging the surfaces.

2. **Lens cleaning solution:** A specialized, non-abrasive cleaning solution designed for optical lenses is recommended. Avoid using general-purpose cleaners, as they may leave residues or damage coatings.

3. **Lens cleaning tissues or swabs:** Optional, for delicate cleaning.

Cleaning the Laser Lens:

1. **Safety Precautions:**
   - Turn off the laser engraving machine and unplug it from the power source before starting the cleaning process. Ensure the laser is completely off.

2. **Access the Lens:**
   - Open the enclosure or access panel to reach the laser lens. Refer to your machine's user manual for guidance on accessing the lens.

3. **Remove Dust and Debris:**
   - Use a can of compressed air to gently blow away loose dust and debris from the lens surface. Hold the can upright and avoid spraying directly onto the lens.

4. **Wet Cleaning:**
   - Apply a small amount of lens cleaning solution to a lint-free laser-safe cleaning cloth. Do not oversaturate the cloth; it should be damp but not dripping.

5. **Clean the Lens:**
   - Gently wipe the lens surface using a circular motion, starting from the center and moving outward. Be very careful not to apply excessive pressure or scratch the lens.

6. **Dry the Lens:**
   - Use a dry, clean part of the cleaning cloth to gently blot and dry the lens. Ensure no cleaning solution or residue remains on the lens.

Cleaning the Mirrors:

1. **Safety Precautions:**
   - Follow the same safety precautions as for cleaning the lens—turn off the machine and disconnect it from the power source.

2. **Access the Mirrors:**
   - Depending on your machine's design, access the mirrors by opening the enclosure or following the manufacturer's instructions.

3. **Remove Dust and Debris:**
   - Use compressed air to blow away loose dust and debris from the mirror surfaces.

4. **Wet Cleaning:**
   - Apply a small amount of lens cleaning solution to a lint-free cleaning cloth or a lens cleaning tissue/swab.

5. **Clean the Mirrors:**

- Gently wipe the mirror surfaces, avoiding excessive pressure. Use a circular motion or follow the manufacturer's recommendations for cleaning direction.

6. **Dry the Mirrors:**

    - Use a dry, clean part of the cleaning cloth or a fresh tissue/swab to gently blot and dry the mirror surfaces. Ensure no cleaning solution or residue remains.

Frequency of Cleaning:

- The frequency of cleaning depends on the level of usage and the operating environment. Regularly inspect the lens and mirrors and clean them as needed. In high-use environments, monthly or even weekly cleaning may be necessary.

Properly maintained and clean optical components are essential for achieving precise and consistent engraving and cutting results. Regularly scheduled maintenance and cleaning will help keep your laser engraving machine operating at its best.

Chapter 8: Advanced Techniques

Photo Engraving

Laser photo engraving, also known as laser photo etching or laser photo engraving, is a specialized application of laser engraving technology that allows you to create highly detailed and realistic engraved images on various materials, including wood, acrylic, glass, metal, and more. This process involves using a laser beam to etch or engrave a photograph or image onto the surface of the material, resulting in a permanent and visually appealing reproduction of the image.

Here are the key steps involved in laser photo engraving:

1. **Image Preparation:**

   - Begin by selecting a high-resolution digital image or photograph. Images with good contrast and sharp details work best for laser photo engraving.

2. **Image Conversion:**

   - Convert the selected image into a format compatible with your laser engraving software. Most laser engraving machines accept common image formats such as JPEG, BMP, PNG, or TIFF.

3. **Software Setup:**

   - Import the image into your laser engraving software, which allows you to adjust and manipulate the image to achieve the desired engraving effect. You can adjust factors such as brightness, contrast, grayscale levels, and dithering to optimize the image for engraving.

4. **Material Selection:**

   - Choose a suitable material for the engraving process. Materials such as wood, acrylic, leather, and certain metals work well for laser photo engraving. The choice of material can impact the final appearance of the engraving.

5. **Machine Setup:**

   - Ensure your laser engraving machine is properly set up for the material you've chosen. This includes configuring laser power, speed, resolution, and focus settings.

6. **Material Preparation:**

   - Place the chosen material on the engraving bed of the machine and secure it in place to prevent movement during the engraving process. Make sure the material is clean and free from debris.

7. **Engraving Process:**

- Start the engraving process by sending the prepared image to the laser engraver. The laser beam will etch the image onto the material's surface pixel by pixel, varying the intensity to create different shades and depths, thereby reproducing the image.

8. **Quality Control:**

- After the engraving is complete, carefully inspect the engraved image for quality and accuracy. Make any necessary adjustments to your settings or image parameters if needed.

9. **Post-Processing:**

- Depending on the material and desired finish, you may choose to add finishing touches to the engraved image, such as applying clear coatings or finishes to enhance contrast or protect the engraving.

10. **Cleaning and Final Presentation:**

- Clean any debris or residue from the engraved material's surface and present the finished laser photo engraving as desired. This could include framing, mounting, or incorporating it into various products or projects.

Laser photo engraving is a versatile and artistic application of laser technology, allowing for the creation of personalized gifts, promotional items, art pieces, and more. The level of detail and realism achievable through this process makes it a popular choice for those looking to add a personal touch to their projects or products.

Speed and Power Settings for Photo Engraving

The speed and power settings for laser photo engraving can vary depending on the type of laser engraving machine you're using, the material you're engraving on, and the desired level of detail and contrast in the photo. Finding the optimal settings may require some experimentation and test engraving to achieve the best results. Here are some general guidelines to consider when setting the speed and power for photo engraving:

1. Material Selection:

- Different materials have different laser interaction properties. The speed and power settings should be adjusted to suit the specific material you're engraving on. Common materials for photo engraving include wood, acrylic, and coated metals.

2. Image Quality and Resolution:

- High-resolution images with good contrast and sharp details generally produce better results. Ensure your photo is well-prepared and optimized for engraving using photo editing software.

3. Initial Test Engraving:

- Begin with a small test engraving on a scrap piece of the same material to determine the optimal settings for your specific laser engraving machine.

4. Power Settings:

- Start with a relatively low power setting (e.g., 10-20% power) and gradually increase it until you achieve the desired engraving depth and darkness. Too much power can result in over-burning or charring, while too little power may produce faint or uneven engraving.

5. Speed Settings:

- Start with a moderate speed setting, such as 400-600 mm/s, and adjust it as needed. Slower speeds can result in more detail and darker engraving, while faster speeds may yield lighter results.

6. Dithering and Halftone Patterns:

- Some laser engraving software allows you to apply dithering or halftone patterns to the image. Experiment with these settings to control the level of detail and shading in the engraving.

7. Grayscale and Multiple Passes:

- Consider engraving in gray-scale mode if your laser engraver supports it. This allows for different shades of gray to be represented by varying laser power levels. Additionally, you can use multiple passes to deepen the engraving and enhance contrast.

8. Image Preprocessing:

- Some laser engraving software provides image preprocessing options, such as contrast adjustment or gamma correction. These adjustments can help optimize the image for engraving.

9. Image Size:

- Larger images may require adjustments to power and speed settings compared to smaller images to maintain consistent engraving quality.

10. Documentation: - Keep records of the settings used for successful photo engravings, as this information can be helpful for future projects.

Remember that the optimal settings can vary from one laser engraving machine to another and depend on the specific material and image you're working with. Be prepared to adjust your settings and conduct test engravings to achieve the best results for your photo engraving projects.

3D Engraving

3D laser engraving, also known as laser 3D engraving or 3D laser etching, is an advanced laser engraving technique that allows you to create intricate three-dimensional designs and patterns on a variety of materials. Unlike traditional 2D engraving, which creates flat images or patterns, 3D laser engraving adds depth and texture to the engraved surface, resulting in a more visually striking and tactile effect.

Here's how 3D laser engraving works and some key considerations:

How 3D Laser Engraving Works:

1. **Laser Scanning:** 3D laser engraving machines are equipped with specialized laser heads that can move both horizontally and vertically. These laser heads emit a focused laser beam.

2. **Surface Mapping:** The laser head moves in a controlled manner over the surface of the material, precisely adjusting the focal point of the laser beam as it moves. It scans the material's surface and creates a topographical map of the area to be engraved.

3. **Depth Control:** During the engraving process, the laser head adjusts the laser's power and intensity based on the topographical data. This allows the laser to remove material at varying depths, creating the 3D effect.

4. **Texture and Relief:** As the laser removes material at different depths, it can create intricate textures, patterns, and reliefs on the material's surface. These textures can mimic natural textures like wood grain or stone, or they can be entirely custom designed.

5. **Complex Designs:** 3D laser engraving can be used to engrave detailed, complex designs, including portraits, logos, sculptures, and more. The level of detail and depth control is determined by the capabilities of the laser engraving machine.

Key Considerations for 3D Laser Engraving:

1. **Material Compatibility:** 3D laser engraving can be performed on various materials, including wood, acrylic, glass, metal, and more. The material's properties, such as hardness and thermal conductivity, may affect the engraving process and results.

2. **Resolution and Detail:** The level of detail and resolution achievable in 3D laser engraving depends on the capabilities of the laser engraving machine, the quality of the laser optics, and the software used for controlling the process.

3. **Image Preparation:** Preparing the design or image for 3D engraving is crucial. Image editing software can be used to convert 2D designs into 3D-ready files, considering depth and texture.

4. **Engraving Depth:** The depth of the engraving is controlled by adjusting the laser's power, speed and the number of passes. Experimentation and test engraving may be necessary to achieve the desired depth and texture.

5. **Safety Precautions:** As with all laser engraving processes, proper safety precautions, including wearing laser safety goggles, should be followed when working with 3D laser engraving machines.

3D laser engraving is commonly used in a wide range of applications, including art and sculpture, product customization, architectural design, and more. It offers a unique and visually striking way to add depth, texture, and intricate details to a variety of objects and materials.

Color Filling Engravings

Color filling laser engravings is a post-processing technique that involves adding color to the engraved areas to enhance the visual impact of the design. This technique is often used to make engraved designs or text stand out and can be particularly effective on materials like wood, acrylic, glass, and certain metals. Here's how you can color fill laser engravings:

Materials and Tools Needed:

1. **Engraved Material:** The item or material with the laser engraving that you want to color fill.

2. **Paint or Ink:** High-quality paint or ink suitable for the material you're working with. Acrylic paint or specialized laser marking inks are commonly used.

3. **Paint Applicator:** A small brush, sponge, or cotton swab for applying the paint or ink.

4. **Masking Tape or Stencil:** To help create clean and precise lines when applying color.

Steps to Color Fill Laser Engravings:

1. **Prepare the Engraving:** Ensure that the laser-engraved design or text is clean and free from any debris or dust. You may need to gently clean the engraved area with a lint-free cloth.

2. **Choose the Paint:** Select the appropriate color of paint or ink that you want to use for color filling. Ensure that the paint is compatible with the material you're working on.

3. **Mask the Surrounding Area (Optional):** If you want to create clean edges and prevent paint from spreading outside the engraved area, you can use masking tape or create a stencil to cover the surrounding surface.

4. **Apply the Paint:**

   - Dip your paint applicator (brush, sponge, or cotton swab) into the paint or ink.

   - Carefully and gently apply the paint to the engraved areas, filling them with color. Take your time to ensure even coverage and avoid overfilling or spilling onto the surrounding material.

- If you're using multiple colors, apply each color one at a time, allowing the previous color to dry before adding the next.

5. **Allow to Dry:** Let the paint or ink dry completely. The drying time will vary depending on the type of paint or ink used, so consult the manufacturer's instructions for guidance.

6. **Remove Masking (If used):** If you used masking tape or a stencil, carefully remove it once the paint is dry.

7. **Clean Up:** Clean your paint applicator and any brushes or tools you use with the appropriate solvent or water, depending on the type of paint or ink.

8. **Sealing (Optional):** To protect the color-filled engraving and enhance its longevity, you can apply a clear sealant or finish compatible with the material. This step is especially important for items that may be handled frequently.

Color filling laser engravings is a creative way to make your designs or messages pop and can be used in various applications, including personalized gifts, signage, artwork, and promotional items. The choice of paint or ink color can significantly impact the final appearance, so experiment with different options to achieve the desired effect.

Rotary Attachments for Laser Engravers

A rotary attachment for laser engraving machines is a specialized accessory that enables the laser engraver to engrave cylindrical or conical objects with precision. These attachments are particularly useful when you need to engrave or mark items like bottles, glasses, mugs, pens, or other curved and cylindrical objects. Here's how a rotary attachment works and its key features:

How a Rotary Attachment Works:

A rotary attachment typically consists of the following components:

1. **Rotary Chuck:** This is a rotating fixture that holds the cylindrical or conical object securely in place during engraving. It can accommodate various diameters and shapes of objects.

2. **Motor and Control:** The rotary attachment includes a motor that rotates the chuck at a controlled and adjustable speed. This motor is connected to the laser engraving machine's control system.

3. **Software Integration:** Laser engraving software that supports rotary attachments allows you to specify the diameter of the object and adjust settings for rotation speed, direction, and positioning.

Here's how a rotary attachment is used:

1. **Mounting the Object:** The object to be engraved is mounted onto the rotary chuck, ensuring it is securely held and properly aligned. The object should be positioned in a way that allows the laser beam to focus on the desired engraving area.

2. **Setting Parameters:** In the laser engraving software, you configure the rotary attachment parameters, including the object's diameter, rotation speed, and the desired position for engraving.

3. **Engraving Process:** When the laser engraving machine is in operation, the rotary attachment rotates the object while the laser head moves along the length of the object. The laser beam engraves the design or text onto the rotating surface.

4. **Precise Engraving:** The rotation of the object ensures that the engraving remains consistent and precise, even on curved or irregularly shaped surfaces.

Key Features and Benefits:

1. **Versatility:** Rotary attachments expand the range of items that can be engraved, allowing for customization of cylindrical objects that would be challenging to engrave with a flatbed engraving table.

2. **Consistent Results:** The rotation of the object ensures that the engraving depth and positioning are consistent, resulting in high-quality and symmetrical engravings.

3. **Ease of Use:** Most modern laser engraving software and machines support rotary attachments, making it relatively straightforward to set up and use.

4. **Wide Range of Applications:** Rotary attachments are used in various industries, including personalization, promotional products, manufacturing, and more.

5. **Customization:** You can engrave logos, text, graphics, and other designs on cylindrical items, making them ideal for branding and personalization purposes.

6. **Timesaving:** Rotary attachments enable batch processing of cylindrical objects, saving time and increasing production efficiency.

7. **Quality Assurance:** The precise control provided by rotary attachments reduces the likelihood of errors, ensuring a professional and polished end product.

Whether you're running a business that offers customized gifts and promotional items or you need to mark cylindrical parts in an industrial setting, a rotary attachment for your laser engraving machine can be a valuable addition, expanding your capabilities and enhancing your engraving options.

Chapter 9: Materials and Applications

Engraving wood and wood products with a laser engraving machine is a popular and versatile application that allows you to create detailed designs, text, and decorative patterns on various types of wood. Whether you're working with solid wood, plywood, MDF (medium-density fiberboard), or wood veneer, laser engraving provides precision and control to achieve impressive results. Here are the steps and considerations for engraving wood:

Materials and Tools Needed:

1. **Laser Engraving Machine:** Ensure that you have access to a laser engraving machine suitable for engraving wood. The machine should have adequate power and a well-focused laser beam.

2. **Wood:** Choose the type of wood that matches your project requirements. Common choices include hardwoods like oak, maple, cherry, or softwoods like pine. You can also engrave plywood, MDF, and other wood-based materials.

3. **Laser Safety Equipment:** Wear appropriate laser safety goggles when operating the machine to protect your eyes from laser light.

Steps for Engraving Wood:

1. **Preparation:**

   - Prepare the wood surface by ensuring it is clean and free from dust, debris, and any contaminants.

2. **Design and File Preparation:**

   - Create or import the design or artwork you want to engrave using graphic design software. Ensure that the design is in a format compatible with your laser engraving software (e.g., vector files like SVG, DXF, or raster images like BMP, JPEG).

3. **Laser Settings:**

   - Set up the laser engraving machine with the appropriate parameters:

     - **Power:** Determine the laser power based on the wood type and the depth of engraving you want. Start with a lower power setting and adjust as needed.

     - **Speed:** Set the engraving speed. Slower speeds generally result in deeper engraving, while faster speeds produce shallower engravings.

- **Resolution:** Choose the engraving resolution (dots per inch or DPI) for detailed or high-quality results. The resolution affects the level of detail in the engraving.
- **Focus:** Ensure the laser beam is focused at the correct depth for optimal engraving results.

4. **Material Placement:**

- Secure the wood piece onto the laser engraving bed. Use clamps or other securing methods to prevent movement during the engraving process.

5. **Engraving:**

- Start the laser engraving process using your prepared design and the specified laser settings. The laser beam will follow the design, removing material to create the engraving.

6. **Quality Control:**

- After engraving is complete, carefully inspect the engraved area for quality and accuracy. Make any necessary adjustments to settings or image parameters if needed.

7. **Post-Processing (Optional):**

- Depending on your project, you may choose to apply finishes, paints, or other treatments to enhance the appearance of the engraved wood.

Considerations:

- **Wood Type:** Different types of wood engrave differently due to variations in density, hardness, and grain patterns. Experiment with settings on scrap wood to determine the best results for your chosen wood type.

- **Depth Control:** Adjust the laser power and speed settings to control the depth of engraving. Lighter settings will produce shallow engravings, while higher power and slower speeds result in deeper engravings.

- **Artwork Optimization:** Optimize your design for engraving by considering factors like contrast, shading, and the level of detail you want to achieve.

- **Ventilation:** Ensure proper ventilation and exhaust systems to remove any smoke or fumes generated during the engraving process.

Engraving wood with a laser provides endless creative possibilities, making it suitable for various applications, including personalized gifts, signage, decorative items, and woodworking projects. By mastering the laser settings and understanding the characteristics of different wood types, you can achieve exceptional results in your engraving projects.

Engraving Metal

Engraving metal with a laser engraving machine is a precise and versatile process that allows you to create detailed designs, text, and markings on various types of metals. Laser engraving is commonly used in industries such as jewelry, aerospace, electronics, and customization of metal products. Here are the steps and considerations for engraving metal:

Materials and Tools Needed:

1. **Laser Engraving Machine:** Ensure you have access to a laser engraving machine equipped with a laser source suitable for engraving metals. Fiber lasers are commonly used for metal engraving due to their high power and precision.

2. **Metal:** Choose the type of metal you want to engrave. Common metals suitable for laser engraving include stainless steel, aluminum, brass, copper, titanium, and more.

3. **Laser Safety Equipment:** Wear appropriate laser safety goggles when operating the machine to protect your eyes from laser light.

Steps for Engraving Metal:

1. **Preparation:**

   - Prepare the metal surface by ensuring it is clean and free from oils, grease, or contaminants. You may need to use a solvent or alcohol to clean the metal surface thoroughly.

2. **Design and File Preparation:**

   - Create or import the design or artwork you want to engrave using graphic design software. Ensure that the design is in a format compatible with your laser engraving software (e.g., vector files like SVG, DXF).

3. **Laser Settings:**

   - Set up the laser engraving machine with the appropriate parameters for metal engraving:

     - **Laser Power:** Determine the laser power based on the type and thickness of the metal. Metals with higher reflectivity may require more power.

     - **Speed:** Set the engraving speed. Slower speeds typically produce deeper engravings, while faster speeds create shallower marks.

     - **Focus:** Ensure the laser beam is focused at the correct depth for optimal engraving results. This is particularly important for metal engraving.

4. **Material Placement:**

- Secure the metal piece onto the laser engraving bed using a work holding system or fixtures to prevent movement during the engraving process.

5. **Engraving:**

- Start the laser engraving process using your prepared design and specified laser settings. The laser beam will follow the design, removing material or creating marks on the metal's surface.

6. **Quality Control:**

- After engraving is complete, carefully inspect the engraved area for quality and accuracy. Make any necessary adjustments to settings or image parameters if needed.

7. **Post-Processing (Optional):**

- Depending on your project, you may choose to apply additional treatments such as coating, polishing, or painting to enhance the appearance of the engraved metal.

Considerations:

- **Metal Type:** Different metals have different characteristics, including hardness and reflectivity, which can affect the engraving process. It's essential to understand how specific metals will react to laser engraving and adjust settings accordingly.

- **Laser Type:** Fiber lasers are commonly used for metal engraving due to their ability to generate high-power laser beams that are well-suited for marking and engraving metals.

- **Depth Control:** Adjust the laser power and speed settings to control the depth of engraving. Lighter settings will produce shallow marks, while higher power and slower speeds can create deeper engravings.

- **Marking and Annealing:** Laser engraving on metal can create a range of effects, including engraving, etching, marking, and annealing. The choice of effect depends on the desired result and the metal type.

Engraving metal with a laser is a precise and efficient process that offers a wide range of applications, from industrial part marking to customizing jewelry and promotional products. Understanding the characteristics of different metals and fine-tuning your laser settings are key to achieving excellent results in metal engraving projects.

Engraving Glass and Acrylic

Engraving glass and acrylic with a laser engraving machine is a versatile and precise process that allows you to create intricate designs, patterns, text, and artwork on these materials. Whether you're working with glass for personalized gifts or acrylic for signage and decorative items, laser engraving provides excellent control and detail. Here are the steps and considerations for engraving glass and acrylic:

Materials and Tools Needed:

1. **Laser Engraving Machine:** Ensure that you have access to a laser engraving machine equipped with a laser source suitable for engraving glass and acrylic. CO2 lasers are commonly used for acrylic, while certain fiber lasers can be used for glass.

2. **Glass or Acrylic:** Select the type of glass or acrylic you want to engrave. Glass options may include clear, colored, or textured glass. Acrylic options may include clear, colored, or cast acrylic sheets.

3. **Laser Safety Equipment:** Wear appropriate laser safety goggles when operating the machine to protect your eyes from laser light.

Steps for Engraving Glass and Acrylic:

1. **Preparation:**

   - Ensure the glass or acrylic surface is clean and free from dust, oils, fingerprints, or contaminants. You may need to use a gentle cleaning solution to ensure a clean surface.

2. **Design and File Preparation:**

   - Create or import the design or artwork you want to engrave using graphic design software. Ensure that the design is in a format compatible with your laser engraving software (e.g., vector files like SVG, DXF).

3. **Laser Settings:**

   - Set up the laser engraving machine with the appropriate parameters for glass or acrylic engraving:

     - **Laser Power:** Determine the laser power based on the material type and thickness. Experiment with power levels to achieve the desired engraving depth and contrast.

     - **Speed:** Set the engraving speed. Slower speeds typically produce deeper engravings, while faster speeds create shallower marks.

     - **Focus:** Ensure the laser beam is focused at the correct depth for optimal engraving results.

4. **Material Placement:**

   - Secure the glass or acrylic piece onto the laser engraving bed using a work holding system or fixtures to prevent movement during the engraving process.

5. **Engraving:**

- Start the laser engraving process using your prepared design and specified laser settings. The laser beam will follow the design, removing material or creating marks on the surface of the glass or acrylic.

6. **Quality Control:**

   - After engraving is complete, carefully inspect the engraved area for quality and accuracy. Make any necessary adjustments to settings or image parameters if needed.

7. **Post-Processing (Optional):**

   - Depending on your project, you may choose to apply additional treatments, such as coating, polishing, or painting, to enhance the appearance of the engraved glass or acrylic.

Considerations:

- **Material Type:** Glass and acrylic have different characteristics that affect the engraving process. Glass engraving is typically done using specialized laser setups, while acrylic engraving is more commonly performed with CO_2 lasers. Understanding these differences is essential for achieving optimal results.

- **Engraving Depth:** Adjust the laser power and speed settings to control the depth of engraving. Lighter settings will produce shallow marks, while higher power and slower speeds can create deeper engravings.

- **Masking:** Applying masking tape or a masking sheet to the surface of glass or acrylic before engraving can help reduce chipping and protect the material during engraving.

- **Etching vs. Engraving:** Depending on your settings, you can create either etched or engraved effects on glass and acrylic. Etching involves creating a frosted or matte finish on the surface, while engraving involves removing material to create deeper and darker marks.

Engraving glass and acrylic with a laser provides a wide range of applications, from personalized gifts and awards to signage, decorative items, and branding. Understanding the characteristics of these materials and fine-tuning your laser settings are crucial for achieving outstanding results in your engraving projects.

Engraving Leather and Fabric

Laser engraving on leather and fabrics is a precise and versatile process that allows you to create intricate designs, patterns, text, and artwork on these materials. Whether you're working with leather for customized accessories or fabrics for textile art, laser engraving provides excellent control and detail. Here are the steps and considerations for laser engraving leather and fabrics:

Materials and Tools Needed:

1. **Laser Engraving Machine:** Ensure you have access to a laser engraving machine equipped with a laser source suitable for engraving leather and fabrics. CO2 lasers are commonly used for these materials.

2. **Leather or Fabric:** Select the type of leather or fabric you want to engrave. Leather options may include genuine leather, synthetic leather, and suede. Fabrics can range from cotton and canvas to polyester and more.

3. **Laser Safety Equipment:** Wear appropriate laser safety goggles when operating the machine to protect your eyes from laser light.

Steps for Laser Engraving Leather and Fabrics:

1. **Preparation:**

   - Ensure the leather or fabric is clean and free from dust, oils, or contaminants. Cleaning may be necessary to ensure a clean surface.

2. **Design and File Preparation:**

   - Create or import the design or artwork you want to engrave using graphic design software. Ensure that the design is in a format compatible with your laser engraving software (e.g., vector files like SVG, DXF).

3. **Laser Settings:**

   - Set up the laser engraving machine with the appropriate parameters for leather or fabric engraving:

     - **Laser Power:** Determine the laser power based on the material type and thickness. Experiment with power levels to achieve the desired engraving depth and contrast.

     - **Speed:** Set the engraving speed. Slower speeds typically produce deeper engravings, while faster speeds create shallower marks.

     - **Focus:** Ensure the laser beam is focused at the correct depth for optimal engraving results.

4. **Material Placement:**

   - Secure the leather or fabric piece onto the laser engraving bed using a work holding system or fixtures to prevent movement during the engraving process. Some fabrics may require masking to reduce scorching or fraying during engraving.

5. **Engraving:**

   - Start the laser engraving process using your prepared design and specified laser setting. The laser beam will follow the design, removing material or creating marks on the surface of the leather or fabric.

6. **Quality Control:**

- After engraving is complete, carefully inspect the engraved area for quality and accuracy. Make any necessary adjustments to settings or image parameters if needed.

7. **Post-Processing (Optional):**

   - Depending on your project, you may choose to apply additional treatments, such as cleaning, finishing, or dyeing, to enhance the appearance of the engraved leather or fabric.

Considerations:

- **Material Type:** Different types of leather and fabrics have varying characteristics, such as thickness, texture, and color, which can affect the engraving process. Conduct tests on scrap material to determine the best settings for your specific material.

- **Engraving Depth:** Adjust the laser power and speed settings to control the depth of engraving. Lighter settings will produce shallow marks, while higher power and slower speeds can create deeper engravings.

- **Masking:** Applying masking tape or a masking sheet to the surface of the material before engraving can help reduce scorching, fraying, or smoke stains on certain fabrics and leather.

- **Design Complexity:** Laser engraving allows for intricate and detailed designs on leather and fabrics, making it ideal for customizing clothing, accessories, home decor, and more.

Laser engraving on leather and fabrics offers a wide range of creative possibilities, from personalizing garments and accessories to adding decorative elements to home textiles and art projects. Understanding the characteristics of these materials and fine-tuning your laser settings are essential for achieving outstanding results in your engraving projects.

What Materials Should You NOT Laser Engrave

Laser engraving is a versatile process, but there are certain materials that should not be laser engraved due to safety concerns, potential damage to the laser system, or the release of harmful fumes. It's important to exercise caution and avoid engraving the following materials:

1. **PVC (Polyvinyl Chloride):** PVC releases chlorine gas when exposed to high temperatures, such as those generated by laser engraving. This gas is highly corrosive and can damage the laser system and pose health risks.

2. **Vinyl and Vinyl-Coated Materials:** Like PVC, vinyl and vinyl-coated materials can release harmful chlorine gas when exposed to laser heat. Avoid engraving vinyl decals, stickers, or vinyl-coated fabrics.

3. **Polycarbonate and Lexan:** Polycarbonate materials release toxic fumes when subjected to laser engraving. These fumes can be harmful to both the laser operator and the machine.

4. **Polystyrene (Styrofoam):** Laser engraving on polystyrene can produce harmful fumes and may cause the material to catch fire due to its flammable nature.

5. **Polyurethane:** Laser engraving on polyurethane foams and coatings can release toxic fumes and create a fire hazard.

6. **Teflon (PTFE):** Engraving on Teflon or PTFE materials can produce harmful fumes and potentially damage the laser system.

7. **Fiberglass:** Engraving fiberglass can release hazardous particles into the air, posing respiratory risks to the operator. Additionally, fiberglass can cause excessive wear on laser optics due to its abrasive nature.

8. **Certain Metals:** While metals like stainless steel and aluminum can be laser engraved with the appropriate laser system, others, like copper and brass, are highly reflective and can damage the laser optics. Always check the compatibility of the metal with your laser engraving machine.

9. **Glass with Certain Coatings:** Some types of coated glass can produce harmful fumes when laser engraved. It's essential to know the composition of the glass and its coating before attempting engraving.

10. **Materials with Unknown Composition:** Avoid engraving materials with unknown compositions, as they may contain substances that can release toxic fumes or pose other safety hazards.

11. **Food:** Laser engraving on food items can introduce contaminants and is not recommended for consumption. It's also important to avoid any materials that could release harmful chemicals when exposed to laser heat.

12. **Materials Containing Asbestos:** Asbestos-containing materials should never be engraved, as the release of asbestos fibers poses severe health risks.

Always consult your laser engraving machine's manufacturer guidelines and safety documentation for a list of compatible and incompatible materials. Additionally, ensure proper ventilation and safety measures are in place when working with any materials to protect both yourself and the laser system from potential hazards.

Chapter 10: Turning Your Hobby into a Business

Turning your laser engraving hobby into a business can be a rewarding venture that allows you to monetize your skills and creativity. Whether you're interested in offering personalized gifts, custom products, or specialized services, here are steps to help you transition from a hobbyist to a laser engraving business owner:

Research and Business Planning:

- **Market Research:** Conduct thorough market research to identify your target audience, competitors, and potential niches within the laser engraving industry. Determine the demand for your services and products.

- **Business Plan:** Create a detailed business plan outlining your business goals, target market, pricing strategy, marketing plan, and financial projections. This plan will serve as your roadmap for success.

Legal Considerations:

- **Business Structure:** Choose a legal structure for your business, such as a sole proprietorship, LLC, or corporation. Consult with legal and tax professionals to determine the best structure for your needs.

- **Business Registration:** Register your business with the appropriate government authorities and obtain any necessary licenses and permits.

- **Insurance:** Consider business insurance, including liability insurance, to protect yourself and your assets in case of accidents or legal issues.

Equipment and Workspace:

- **Acquire Equipment:** Invest in high-quality laser engraving equipment suitable for your intended applications and volume of work. Consider factors like laser power, bed size, and additional features.

- **Workspace:** Set up a dedicated workspace that complies with safety regulations and allows for efficient production. Ensure proper ventilation and safety measures are in place.

Material Sourcing:

- **Source Materials:** Establish relationships with suppliers to procure the materials you'll need for engraving, such as wood, acrylic, metal, leather, and more.

- **Quality Control:** Ensure the materials you use are of high quality to deliver excellent results to your customers.

Product and Service Offerings:

- **Define Your Niche:** Determine the specific products or services you'll offer. This could include personalized gifts, signage, promotional items, or industrial engraving services.

- **Pricing Strategy:** Set competitive and profitable prices for your offerings. Consider factors such as material costs, labor, overhead, and market demand.

Branding and Marketing:

- **Branding:** Create a strong brand identity, including a business name, logo, and branding materials that reflect your style and professionalism.

- **Online Presence:** Build a professional website showcasing your work, services, pricing, and contact information. Use social media platforms to promote your business and engage with potential customers.

- **Networking:** Attend local business networking events and trade shows to connect with potential clients and partners.

Legal and Financial Management:

- **Contracts:** Develop clear contracts or agreements for your clients that outline pricing, terms, and delivery schedules.

- **Financial Management:** Set up a dedicated business bank account to separate personal and business finances. Use accounting software to track income, expenses, and taxes.

Customer Service:

- **Excellent Service:** Provide exceptional customer service to build trust and secure repeat business. Respond promptly to inquiries and address customer concerns promptly.

Scaling Your Business:

- **Hire Help:** As your business grows, consider hiring employees or outsourcing certain tasks to manage increased demand.

- **Diversify:** Explore additional revenue streams, such as offering related products or services, to diversify your income.

Compliance and Regulations:

- **Compliance:** Stay informed about industry regulations, safety standards, and any changes in tax laws that may affect your business.

Quality Control:

- **Maintain Quality:** Continuously strive for high-quality work to build a positive reputation and gain referrals.

Starting a laser engraving business can be a rewarding endeavor, but it's important to approach it with a solid plan, dedication, and a focus on quality and customer satisfaction. With the right strategy and commitment, you can turn your hobby into a successful and profitable business.

Pricing your Engraving Services

Pricing your engraving services effectively is crucial to the success and sustainability of your laser engraving business. It's essential to strike a balance between covering your costs, earning a profit, and offering competitive prices to attract customers. Here's a step-by-step guide to help you determine the pricing structure for your engraving services:

1. Calculate Your Costs:

- **Materials:** Determine the cost of materials used for each project, including the engraving substrate (wood, acrylic, metal, etc.) and any additional materials like paint, coatings, or adhesives.

- **Labor:** Estimate the amount of time you spend on each project, including design preparation, setup, and engraving. Calculate labor costs based on an hourly rate that reflects your skill level and experience.

- **Overhead:** Consider your business overhead expenses, such as rent, utilities, equipment maintenance, insurance, software subscriptions, and marketing costs. Divide your annual overhead by the number of projects you anticipate completing to determine the overhead cost per project.

- **Profit Margin:** Decide on a reasonable profit margin that you want to earn for your business. Typically, a profit margin of 20% to 50% is considered standard for most industries.

2. Research Your Competition:

- Investigate what your competitors are charging for similar engraving services in your local market. This can give you a benchmark for pricing your own services.

- Pay attention to the quality of work, materials used, and additional services offered by competitors. Your pricing should reflect the value you provide relative to your competition.

3. Consider Market Demand:

- Assess the demand for your engraving services in your target market. Are there specific niches or industries with higher demand? Price adjustments may be needed based on the level of competition and market saturation.

4. Determine Pricing Strategies:

- **Fixed Pricing:** Set standard prices for common engraving services that are easy for customers to understand. For example, you might charge a fixed rate for engraving a nameplate or a specific-sized sign.

- **Tiered Pricing:** Create pricing tiers based on the complexity, size, or customization level of projects. Customers can choose the tier that best matches their needs and budget.

- **Custom Quotes:** For highly customized or one-of-a-kind projects, provide individualized quotes based on the specific requirements, materials, and design complexity.

5. Pricing Models:

- **Hourly Rate:** Calculate your hourly rate based on your labor costs and desired profit margin. This model is suitable for projects where the time required can vary significantly.

- **Per Square Inch or Per Square Foot:** Charge based on the surface area of the engraving. This model is often used for engraving on materials like wood or acrylic.

- **Per Piece:** Set a fixed price for each item or product engraved. This model works well for projects with consistent sizes and complexity levels.

6. Test and Adjust:

- Start with your calculated pricing, but be open to adjustments based on customer feedback, market conditions, and your own experience. Regularly review and update your pricing strategy as needed.

7. Offer Value-Added Services:

- Consider offering additional services, such as design customization, rush orders, or packaging, for an additional fee. This can help increase your revenue and cater to a wider range of customer needs.

8. Communicate Your Pricing Clearly:

- Ensure that your pricing is transparent and easy for customers to understand. Clearly list your rates on your website, promotional materials, and quotes.

9. Track Your Financials:

- Keep accurate records of your income, expenses, and profit margins. This will help you assess the profitability of your pricing strategy and make informed adjustments as needed.

Remember that pricing is not set in stone, and it may evolve as your business grows and market dynamics change. Regularly evaluate your pricing strategy to ensure it remains competitive and profitable while meeting the needs of your customers.

Legal Considerations
When operating a laser engraving business, there are several legal considerations to be aware of to ensure that you comply with relevant laws and regulations and protect both your business and your customers. Here are some key legal considerations when laser engraving:

1. Business Structure and Registration:

- Choose a legal structure for your business, such as a sole proprietorship, LLC (Limited Liability Company), or corporation. Register your business and obtain any necessary permits and licenses based on your location and business type.

2. Contracts and Agreements:

- Create clear and comprehensive contracts or agreements for your customers. These contracts should outline the scope of work, pricing, payment terms, delivery dates, and any other terms and conditions relevant to your laser engraving services.

3. Intellectual Property Rights:

- Respect intellectual property rights. Do not engrave copyrighted designs, logos, or artwork without the proper authorization or licensing. Be aware of trademarked or copyrighted materials that clients provide for engraving.

4. Product Liability and Safety:

- Ensure the safety of your products. If you are producing engraved items, especially those intended for use or display, make sure they meet safety standards and do not pose any hazards to consumers.

5. Environmental and Health Regulations:

- Comply with environmental and health regulations. If your laser engraving materials or processes produce fumes or hazardous waste, you may need to adhere to specific regulations regarding ventilation, waste disposal, and air quality control.

6. Privacy and Data Protection:

- Protect customer data. If your business collects personal information from customers, implement data protection measures to safeguard sensitive data and comply with privacy laws such as the General Data Protection Regulation (GDPR) in Europe or the California Consumer Privacy Act (CCPA).

7. Taxation:

- Understand your tax obligations. Keep accurate financial records, report your income, and pay taxes on time. Consult with an accountant or tax professional to ensure compliance with local, state, and federal tax laws.

8. Product Labeling and Compliance:

- Ensure that engraved products, especially those sold to consumers, meet labeling and compliance requirements. This may include disclosing materials used, providing care instructions, and complying with safety regulations.

9. Liability Insurance:

- Consider obtaining liability insurance to protect your business from potential legal claims or lawsuits. This type of insurance can cover costs associated with legal defense and settlement in case of accidents, injuries, or product defects.

10. Copyright and Trademark for Your Business:

- Protect your business's intellectual property by registering trademarks and copyrights for your business name, logo, and any unique designs or artwork you create.

11. Permits and Local Regulations:

- Check for any specific local regulations or zoning requirements that may apply to your business location. These regulations can affect issues like signage, business hours, and operating from a residential area.

12. Shipping and Export Restrictions:

- Be aware of any restrictions on shipping engraved items, especially internationally. Some items may be subject to export controls or import restrictions in certain countries.

13. Dispute Resolution:

- Establish a dispute resolution process in your contracts or terms of service to address potential conflicts with customers. This can help resolve issues without the need for legal action.

It's important to consult with legal professionals or business advisors who specialize in your industry or locality to ensure that you are in compliance with all relevant laws and regulations. Staying informed and proactive in addressing legal considerations can help you operate your laser engraving business smoothly while minimizing legal risks.

Chapter 11: Frequently Asked Questions of Laser Engravers

Frequently Asked Questions (FAQs) can be a valuable resource for customers and clients looking to understand your laser engraving services and address common concerns. Here are some frequently asked questions and sample answers that you can consider for your laser engraving business:

1. What is laser engraving, and how does it work?

- Laser engraving is a precise and versatile process that uses a high-powered laser beam to create detailed designs, text, and patterns on various materials. The laser removes or marks the material's surface to create the desired image or text.

2. What materials can be laser engraved?

- Laser engraving is compatible with a wide range of materials, including wood, acrylic, metal, glass, leather, fabric, and more. The choice of material depends on the project's requirements and the desired outcome.

3. What types of projects can you do with laser engraving?

- We can handle a variety of projects, including personalized gifts, signage, promotional products, awards, industrial part marking, and custom artwork on various materials.

4. Can you engrave photographs and detailed graphics?

- Yes, we can engrave detailed graphics and photographs, provided that the image files are high-resolution and suitable for laser engraving. Complex designs may require additional setup and may affect pricing.

5. Is laser engraving permanent?

- Laser engraving creates permanent marks on the material's surface. However, the longevity of the engraving can vary depending on the material and environmental factors.

6. How do I place an order for laser engraving services?

- To place an order, simply contact us via phone, email, or our website. Provide details about your project, including material, design, quantity, and any specific requirements. We will provide you with a quote and timeline.

7. What is the turnaround time for laser engraving orders?

- Turnaround times vary depending on the complexity of the project and our current workload. We will provide you with an estimated delivery date when you place your order.

8. Do you offer bulk or wholesale pricing for large orders?

- Yes, we offer bulk and wholesale pricing for large orders. Contact us with the details of your project, including the quantity, and we will provide you with a customized quote.

9. Can you engrave on customer-provided items or materials?

- In many cases, we can engrave on customer-provided items or materials. However, we may need to assess the material's compatibility and condition before proceeding.

10. Is laser engraving safe for food-related items or baby products?

Laser engraving is safe for food-related items and baby products when appropriate materials and methods are used. Ensure that all materials used meet safety standards and are laser safe.

11. How can I care for and maintain engraved items?

Engraved items can be cleaned with a gentle, non-abrasive cloth or sponge. Avoid harsh chemicals or abrasive cleaners that could damage the engraving. Do not put into dishwashers engraved products.

12. Do you offer shipping and delivery services?

You will determine based on your pricing whether you want to include shipping and delivery services as an all-in cost.

13. What file formats are compatible with your laser engraving system?

A range of file formats, including vector files (SVG, DXF, AI) and high-resolution raster images (JPEG, PNG, BMP). Use the format that best suits the design.

14. Is laser engraving eco-friendly?

Laser engraving is considered an environmentally friendly process as it produces minimal waste and emissions.

These FAQs can serve as a starting point for addressing common inquiries from your customers. Customize your FAQs to reflect your specific services, materials, and business policies to provide clear and informative answers to potential clients.

Chapter 12: Resources and Further Learning

If you're interested in laser engraving and want to learn more, improve your skills, or start a laser engraving business, there are several valuable resources available. Here's a list of resources that can help you get started and excel in the world of laser engraving:

1. Online Communities and Forums:

- **Laser Engraver Subreddit:** The r/laserengraving subreddit is a great place to connect with other laser enthusiasts, ask questions, and share your work.

- **Trotec Laser Forum:** Trotec, a laser machine manufacturer, has an active forum where users discuss laser engraving techniques and troubleshooting.

2. Laser Engraving Books:

- "Laser Processing of Engineering Materials" by C. Suryanarayana and M. A. Meyers: This book covers various aspects of laser processing, including engraving, cutting, and welding.

- "Laser Engraving for the Woodworker" by Bruce Richardson: This book focuses on laser engraving techniques specifically for woodworking.

3. YouTube Channels and Tutorials:

- **Epilog Laser:** Epilog, a laser engraving machine manufacturer, offers informative tutorials and how-to videos on their YouTube channel.

- **Trotec Laser:** Trotec also provides instructional videos covering a wide range of laser engraving topics.

- **Boss Laser:** Boss Laser's YouTube channel offers tutorials, project ideas, and tips for laser engraving.

4. Online Courses:

- **Udemy:** Udemy offers various online courses related to laser engraving, including beginner to advanced levels.

- **LinkedIn Learning (formerly Lynda.com):** You can find courses on laser engraving and related topics, such as graphic design and materials, on LinkedIn Learning.

5. Laser Machine Manufacturers:

- Visit the websites of laser engraving machine manufacturers like Epilog, Trotec, Boss Laser, and Universal Laser Systems for informative resources, webinars, and guides.

6. Local Maker Spaces and Fab Labs:

- Check if there are any maker spaces or fab labs in your area that offer access to laser engraving equipment and training.

7. Online Retailers:

- Websites like Amazon and eBay offer a wide range of laser engraving materials, supplies, and accessories that can help you with your projects.

8. Laser Engraving Software:

- Learn how to use laser engraving software like Adobe Illustrator, CorelDRAW, RDWorks, and LightBurn. Many of these software programs offer tutorials and guides.

9. Trade Shows and Workshops:

- Attending industry trade shows and workshops to stay updated on the latest laser engraving technologies and techniques.

10. Local Laser Engraving Businesses:

- Connect with local laser engraving businesses and inquire about opportunities for mentorship, training, or collaboration.

11. Online Stores and Marketplaces:

- Websites like Etsy and eBay can serve as sources of inspiration, allowing you to see what types of laser-engraved products are popular and how they're priced.

12. Social Media and Online Communities:

- Platforms like Instagram, Pinterest, and Facebook have numerous laser engraving communities and pages where you can find inspiration, tips, and connect with other enthusiasts.

13. Equipment Manuals and Documentation:

- If you own a specific laser engraving machine, consult the manufacturer's website for equipment manuals, software guides, and troubleshooting resources.

14. Industry Publications:

- Subscribe to industry magazines and publications like "Laser Focus World" and "Industrial Laser Solutions" to stay informed about the latest developments in laser technology.

These resources offer a wealth of information for both beginners and experienced laser engravers, helping you expand your knowledge and skills in this exciting field. Whether you're pursuing laser engraving as a hobby or a business, continuous learning and staying up to date with industry trends are key to your success.

Suppliers and Materials

Finding the right materials suppliers for laser engraving can greatly impact the quality and success of your engraving projects. Here are some recommended materials suppliers that offer a wide range of materials suitable for laser engraving:

1. Johnson Plastics Plus:

- Website: Johnson Plastics Plus

- Johnson Plastics Plus offers a variety of laser engraving materials, including acrylic sheets, wood, metal, plastic, and more. They also provide tools and accessories for engraving.

2. Trotec Materials:

- Website: Trotec Materials

- Trotec offers a selection of laser engraving materials specifically designed for their laser systems. Their product range includes acrylics, woods, metals, and laminates.

3. Rowmark:

- Website: Rowmark

- Rowmark is known for its high-quality plastic materials designed for laser engraving and rotary engraving. They offer a wide range of color options and finishes.

4. JDS Industries:

- Website: JDS Industries

- JDS Industries provides various materials and supplies for laser engraving, including acrylics, wood, metal, and sublimation products. They also offer custom fabrication services.

5. Gravotech:

- Website: Gravotech Materials

- Gravotech offers a selection of materials suitable for laser engraving, such as plastics, metals, and laminates. They provide detailed product information and specifications.

6. LaserBits:

- Website: LaserBits

- LaserBits offers laser engraving materials, tools, and accessories. They have a wide range of materials, including acrylics, wood, glass, and metals.

7. 2PO (Two Point Zero):

- Website: 2PO

- 2PO specializes in laser engraving materials, particularly for photo engraving. They offer a variety of materials and finishes designed for high-quality photo reproduction.

8. Amazon and eBay:

- Online marketplaces like Amazon and eBay offer a wide selection of laser engraving materials, including acrylic sheets, wood blanks, metal plates, and more. Ensure that the materials you purchase are compatible with laser engraving.

9. Local Suppliers:

- Consider checking with local plastics suppliers, hardware stores, and specialty material shops for laser engraving materials. They may carry acrylic sheets, wood, and other materials suitable for engraving.

10. Specialty Suppliers: - Depending on your specific engraving needs, you may also find specialty suppliers for certain materials. For instance, if you focus on leather engraving, look for leather suppliers that offer laser-compatible leather products.

When choosing a materials supplier, it's essential to consider factors such as material quality, availability, pricing, and shipping options. Additionally, some suppliers may offer sample packs or swatches, allowing you to test materials before making larger purchases.

Glossary of Laser Engraving Terms

Here is a glossary of laser engraving terms to help you understand key concepts and terminology related to laser engraving:

1. Laser Engraving:

- The process of using a high-powered laser beam to etch, mark, or engrave materials, creating precise and detailed designs or text.

2. Laser Engraving Machine:

- A device equipped with a laser source used to perform laser engraving on various materials.

3. Laser Source:

- The component of a laser engraving machine that generates the laser beam used for engraving. Common types include CO_2 lasers and fiber lasers.

4. CO2 Laser:

- A type of laser source that uses carbon dioxide gas as the lasering medium to produce a laser beam. CO_2 lasers are commonly used for engraving materials like wood, acrylic, and glass.

5. Fiber Laser:

- A type of laser source that uses optical fibers as the lasing medium. Fiber lasers are known for their high energy efficiency and are often used for metal engraving.

6. Engraving Depth:

- The depth to which the laser beam penetrates the material during the engraving process, determining the mark's depth.

7. Raster Engraving:

- A method of engraving where the laser moves back and forth in a raster pattern to create shading or filled areas in an image.

8. Vector Engraving:

- A method of engraving where the laser follows the outlines of vector graphics, such as text or line art, resulting in precise and sharp lines.

9. DPI (Dots Per Inch):

- A measurement of image resolution that determines the level of detail in an engraving. Higher DPI values result in finer details.

10. Kerf: - The width of material removed by the laser during cutting or engraving. It varies depending on the laser's focal point and material properties.

11. Masking: - The process of applying masking tape or sheets to the material's surface before engraving to protect it from smoke, scorching, or residue.

12. Laminates: - Layered materials often used in laser engraving, such as plastic laminates or layered wood, where the top layer is engraved to reveal a different color underneath.

13. Focal Length: - The distance between the laser lens and the material's surface, affecting the laser's focus and engraving quality.

14. Halftone: - A technique used in laser engraving to simulate shades of gray or color by varying the dot density in a pattern of small dots.

15. Backlash: - The small amount of play or movement in the mechanical components of a laser engraving machine, which can affect engraving accuracy.

16. LPI (Lines Per Inch): - A measurement that determines the spacing of lines in halftone or dithered patterns, affecting the engraving's texture.

17. Dithering: - A technique used to simulate shades or gradients in laser engraving by arranging dots in different patterns.

18. Beam Expander: - An optical component that expands the laser beam to achieve a larger spot size and increased power density.

19. Ventilation System: - A system that removes fumes, smoke, and airborne particles generated during laser engraving to maintain a safe and clean working environment.

20. Fume Extractor: - A device that captures and filters fumes and particulates produced during laser engraving to improve air quality.

1. CNC (Computer Numerical Control): - The automated control of a machine tool or process using a computer to execute precise and repeatable operations, commonly used in laser engraving machines.

his glossary should provide you with a foundational understanding of laser engraving terminology. As ou delve deeper into laser engraving, you may encounter additional specialized terms and concepts elated to specific materials and techniques.

Chapter 13 Conclusion

The Joy of Laser Engraving

The joy of laser engraving lies in the combination of creativity, precision, and the tangible results of your work. Here are some aspects of laser engraving that enthusiasts and professionals find fulfilling and enjoyable:

1. Creative Expression: Laser engraving allows you to transform your ideas and designs into tangible objects. Whether you're creating personalized gifts, intricate artwork, or custom signage, it's a medium for artistic expression.

2. Precision and Detail: Laser engraving machines offer exceptional precision and detail. You can achieve intricate designs, fine lines, and complex patterns that may be challenging to replicate by hand.

3. Versatility: Laser engraving can be applied to a wide range of materials, from wood and acrylic to metal, glass, and even fabrics. This versatility opens up endless possibilities for projects and experimentation.

4. Personalization: Engraving allows you to add a personal touch to items, making them unique and meaningful. Whether it's engraving names, dates, or special messages, you can create one-of-a-kind gifts and keepsakes.

5. Business Opportunities: For entrepreneurs, the joy of laser engraving extends to the satisfaction of building a successful business. It's a niche with growing demand, and the ability to turn your hobby into a profitable venture can be incredibly rewarding.

6. Problem Solving: Laser engraving often involves overcoming challenges, such as optimizing settings for different materials or troubleshooting machine issues. The process of problem-solving and continuous improvement can be fulfilling.

7. Learning and Skill Development: Laser engraving requires learning about materials, machine settings, and design software. Acquiring and honing these skills can be intellectually stimulating and personally satisfying.

8. Seeing Your Vision Come to Life: There's a unique joy in witnessing your designs take shape as the laser interacts with the material. It's a hands-on process where you have control over the outcome.

9. Efficiency: Laser engraving is an efficient way to create detailed engravings, especially for repetitive tasks. It can save time and labor compared to traditional engraving methods.

10. Community and Sharing: Engaging with the laser engraving community, whether through forums, social media, or local maker spaces, allows you to share your passion, learn from others, and gain inspiration from their work.

11. Eco-Friendly Option: Laser engraving is often considered an eco-friendly option because it produces minimal waste and emissions compared to some other manufacturing and engraving methods.

12. Business Growth and Innovation: For those running laser engraving businesses, the joy comes from watching your business grow and innovating to meet customer demands. You can continuously expand your offerings and explore new markets.

In summary, the joy of laser engraving stems from the blend of creativity, precision, and versatility it offers. Whether you're a hobbyist or a professional, laser engraving provides a fulfilling outlet for artistic expression, problem-solving, and the opportunity to turn your passion into a thriving venture.

Encouragement for Future Engravers

If you're considering becoming a laser engraver or you've just started your journey in laser engraving, here's some encouragement to help you along the way:

1. Embrace the Learning Process:

- Laser engraving is a skill that takes time to master. Don't be discouraged by initial challenges or mistakes. Every engraver, whether novice or expert, started as a beginner. Embrace the learning process and view each project as an opportunity to improve.

2. Start Small, Dream Big:

- Begin with simple projects and gradually work your way up to more complex designs and materials. As you gain confidence and experience, you'll be amazed at what you can accomplish. Your skills will grow with each engraving.

3. Explore Your Creativity:

- Laser engraving is a medium for creative expression. Don't be afraid to experiment, try new techniques, and push the boundaries of your imagination. Your unique ideas and designs can set you apart in the world of engraving.

4. Learn from Others:

- Join laser engraving communities, forums, and social media groups. Engage with experienced engravers, ask questions, and seek advice. Learning from others' experiences and sharing your own can be both educational and inspiring.

5. Stay Patient and Persistent:

- Laser engraving can sometimes be challenging, but persistence is key to success. If you encounter difficulties, take a step back, troubleshoot, and keep trying. The satisfaction of overcoming obstacles is a valuable part of the journey.

6. Celebrate Small Wins:

- Recognize and celebrate your achievements, no matter how small they may seem. Completing a project, mastering a new technique, or receiving positive feedback from a customer are all milestones worth celebrating.

7. Focus on Quality:

- Quality work is the foundation of a successful engraving business. Pay attention to details, invest in high-quality materials, and continuously strive to improve the quality of your engravings. Customers value craftsmanship.

8. Build Your Brand:

- If you're considering turning your passion into a business, focus on building a strong brand identity. Create a professional website, showcase your work, and develop a reputation for delivering exceptional service and products.

9. Stay Inquisitive:

- The world of laser engraving is ever evolving. Stay curious and open to new techniques, materials, and technologies. Being adaptable and willing to learn will keep your skills fresh and your work exciting.

10. Enjoy the Process: - Ultimately, the joy of laser engraving comes from the process itself. Relish the moments when you see your designs come to life and take pride in the unique creations you produce.

Remember that every engraver started with their first engraving, and the journey is a continuous path of growth and discovery. Whether you're engraving for personal enjoyment or pursuing it as a profession, your passion and dedication will lead to fulfilling results. Keep your enthusiasm alive, and the world of laser engraving will remain an exciting and rewarding endeavor.

MATERIALS SPEED AND POWER CHART GUIDE

Creating a speed and power materials chart for laser engraving is a valuable resource for laser engravers. However, it's important to note that the ideal speed and power settings can vary depending on the specific laser machine, its wattage, the lens used, and the material being engraved. Below is a generalized chart to give you an idea of starting points for some common materials. You should always conduct test engravings to fine-tune settings for your specific setup and achieve the desired results.

Material	Speed (%)	Power (%)	DPI (Dots Per Inch)
Wood (Plywood)	50-70%	20-40%	500-1000 DPI
Acrylic	30-60%	50-70%	600-1000 DPI
Glass	20-30%	70-80%	600-1000 DPI
Metal (Coated/Anodized)	20-40%	80-100%	600-1000 DPI
Leather	40-60%	20-40%	600-1000 DPI
Fabric (Cotton)	30-50%	15-30%	500-1000 DPI
Paper	50-70%	20-40%	600-1000 DPI
Cardstock	50-70%	20-40%	600-1000 DPI
Rubber	30-50%	40-60%	600-1000 DPI
Cork	40-60%	20-40%	600-1000 DPI

Keep in mind that this chart provides only general starting points. To determine the optimal settings for a specific material, follow these steps:

1. Conduct Test Engravings: Begin with a small test piece of the material you intend to engrave. Use a range of speed and power settings and vary the DPI to find the best combination for your desired effect.

2. Observe Results: Inspect the test engravings to evaluate the depth, clarity, and overall quality of the engraving. Pay attention to any charring or scorching on the material.

3. Make Adjustments: Based on your observations, make incremental adjustments to the speed and power settings until you achieve the desired result. Take note of the settings that work best for each material type.

4. Document Findings: Keep a record of your settings and results for future reference. This will help streamline the process for future engraving projects on similar materials.

5. Consider Material Thickness: Material thickness can also impact the optimal settings. Adjustments may be necessary when engraving thicker or thinner materials.

6. Lens and Focal Length: Different lenses and focal lengths can influence the engraving outcome. Experiment with these factors as well if you have the option.

Remember that laser engraving is both an art and a science, and it often involves a degree of trial and error. Over time, you'll develop a deeper understanding of how different materials react to varying speed and power settings, allowing you to achieve precise and consistent results.

Made in the USA
Middletown, DE
23 November 2024

65300447R00056